EDUCATING
AN
ENGLISTANEE
...INSHALLAH

CHARLES LEIGH

Matador
9 Priory Business Park
Kibworth Beauchamp
Leicestershire LE8 0RX, UK
Tel: (+44) 116 279 2299
Fax: (+44) 116 279 2277
Email: books@troubador.co.uk
Web: www.troubador.co.uk/matador

ISBN 978 1848766 747

British Library Cataloguing in Publication Data.
A catalogue record for this book is available from the British Library.

Typeset in Palatino by Troubador Publishing Ltd, Leicester, UK
Printed and bound in the UK by TJ International, Padstow, Cornwall

Matador is an imprint of Troubador Publishing Ltd

In the memory of

Rupert Montague Leigh - 17th April 1912 - 3rd December 2004

Michael Donald Kyrle-Pope - 1st October 1916 - 14th September 2008

All the author's proceeds from *Educating an Englistanee... Inshallah* will be donated to the inter faith dialogue and conflict resolution charity, Foundation for Relief and Reconciliation in the Middle East.

Acknowledgements

Due to the often dangerous and difficult lives of many I have met during my travels clockwise around the Middle East, those whom I most need to thank remain anonymous under a different name to protect their true identity. I can only thank them by recalling within this book the kindness and generosity shown to me within their homes, where more often than not, the Arab welcome: *Baity Baitak* (my house is your house) was heard.

This project started during afternoons in the school library avoiding rugby training. Firstly the Headmaster of Blundell's School, Ian Davenport has been continuously supportive, together with his colleagues Tim Dyke, Tim Hunt, Andrew Berrow and Paddy Armstrong. A special thank you must go to the Head of the Art Department, Bertie Matthews and his pupil, Lauren Kalsi, for her wonderful illustrations. As an alumnus of Blundell's School, Father Nilus must be thanked for allowing me to stay at St Catherine's Monastery for three unforgettable days. I also thank Robert Fisk for his generosity and encouragement. Many thanks to Susie Bond, who has been very generous in all efforts of proof reading and editing.

I would also thank family and friends for their support and encouragement. My parents, Jonathan and Emma Leigh have had to endure a never ending pile of proofs to read along with my sister, Issy, grandmother, Suzanne Kyrle-Pope and uncle, James Kyrle-Pope. Julie Wimbush, my Godmother, has gone beyond the pale in having me to stay for so long during the wilderness months. Lastly, I could not have completed this without the advice and support of Adam Holloway, John Deverell, Peter Cameron and Juliet Wurr.

Contents

Preface   *ix*

Module 1: Government and governance   1

The *Animal Farm* case study – Tehran, Iran   3
The tale of two Hosnis – Cairo, Egypt   14
Thieves of Democracy – Aden, Yemen   21
A nation's desire for democracy? – Sana'a, Yemen   26
Drinking with soldiers: A toast to freedom? –
Jerusalem, Israel and the Palestinian Territories   30
The Cedar Revolution – Beirut, Lebanon.   39
Trolls in the mist. Great Arab conspiracy theories –
Aleppo, Syria   51

Module 2: Minorities in the region   57

Mehvec Kenan and the Kurdish 'problem' –
Diyarbakir, Turkey   59
The Palestinian refugees of Shatila –Beirut, Lebanon   68
Jerusalem and Khalid Kateb -
Jerusalem, Israel and the Palestinian territories   81

Module 3: Religion   87

Mashad. The city of martyrs – Iran   89
35 Lashes for a bottle – Isfahan, Iran   95
Sleeping Carlos and the Greeks – Sinai, Egypt   104
The changing colours of a metaphorical taxi –
Beirut, Lebanon   123

Module 4: An introduction to Economics   **129**

Migration trends: Bandar Abbas to Bangkok and back –
Bander Abbas, Persian Gulf, Iran   131
Labour Movement: Dubai and the race based economy –
Dubai, United Arab Emirates   135
The Green agenda: One man's rubbish is another's treasure -
Cairo, Egypt   141
Economic inequality: The guilt of giving –
Aden, Yemen   145

Module 5: Sex Education   **149**

Escaping sodomy – Tabriz, Iran   151
Sex and death in provincial Syria – Dayr as Zawr, Syria   157
A Phoenician transvestite –Beirut, Lebanon   165

Module 6: General Studies   **169**

Marmite and American identity.
A dichotomy of love and hatred – Sana'a, Yemen   171
Two people come to terms with death – Aden, Yemen   178
10 seconds for 43,000 lives – Bam, Iran   181
Fadhi from a better life in Falluja – Muscat, Oman   187
Entering Yemen with Julia Roberts – Al-Hawf, Yemen   192

Final Exam   **203**

Failing the assessment: drinks with Robert Fisk –
Beirut, Lebanon   205

When giving the speech one Prize Day at Blundell's where not only Charles Leigh was educated but also Richard Blackmore author of Lorna Doone, I told the graduating year to "Go East"! Charles Leigh must have paid attention to what I was saying for indeed he did this in a most spectacular way.

Educating an Englistanee....Inshallah is Charlie's account of all you might wish to find, and a lot more beside, if you yourself set out with a simple back-pack to explore the part of the world roughly between the Eastern shores of the Mediterranean, the Southern shores of the Caspian, the hub of the Persian Gulf, and the North Western shores of the Indian ocean. On a limited budget Charlie sees the sides of local life often missed by the usual affluent tourist. He deals with bedbugs and obstructive immigration officials with equanimity. His greatest challenges, however, are clearly to himself. He strives to cope with loneliness, uncertainty and disillusionment in discovering that what he has learnt and accepted as "truth" in newspapers and textbooks about the socio-political complexities of these various countries does not begin to cover the interweaving layers of problems which beset the different nations. The images portrayed by the Western media bear no relation to the reality in front of him. There is no black and white and never likely to be so.

Charles Leigh writes with humour and warmth as he describes those with whom he comes into contact. Clearly they leave a marked impression on him as this book will leave on its readers. If the West is to comprehend and deal with the increasing number of problems arising from this part of the world, I would urge people to read this and follow Charlie's example to discover for themselves a greater understanding of the indigenous peoples and what makes them who they are.

This area will continue to dominate world politics for most of the twenty-first century. It is vital that the next generation comes to terms with the great opportunity of walking, as Charlie does, in the steps of the very people from whom we have so much to comprehend. Only through connecting can the next generation realise the aspiration to make the globe a better place where positive levels of mutual regard and co-operation shine through.

Sir Christopher Ondaatje OC OBE

This is an ambitious book for an 18-year old author and he has managed it brilliantly, covering issues of great complexity in a region often plagued by its long and tormented history.

Sir Ranulph Fiennes OBE

This book charts Charlie's complex journey from adolescence to manhood, amid the complexities of life in the Middle East. As the months and years pass, this young adventurer begins to look beyond his preconceptions about the region's conflicts, and to see the simple humanity in the midst of it all. He comes to the realisation that befalls all who work for peace here; there are no easy answers.

Canon Dr Andrew White
President of the Foundation for Relief and Reconciliation in the Middle East

Preface

This is a book without agenda other than a search to find the elusive truth. It is not a chronological account of an adolescent's wanderings in the Middle East. It is an improvised text book, a source of reference for experiences which in the most precarious and yet comprehensible of ways relate to central topics.

It is a book of awakening. It is an account of a vagabond school boy who in bouts of ingenuous enthusiasm sets himself a challenge in 2005 to travel overland, clockwise from Istanbul to Jerusalem. It is a journey in two parts into the unknown, a journey beyond the confines of private school and the perceived certainties of the wider West at a particular moment.

It is a story of an eighteen year old trying to reason with the world he sees before him, *yet it is a story that exposes why the Middle East is changing today, and why the bulging youth of the region are rising up and demanding equality and freedom.*

The names of all individuals in this book have been changed for their safety.

إِنَّ ٱلَّذِينَ ءَامَنُوا۟ وَٱلَّذِينَ هَادُوا۟ وَٱلنَّصَـٰرَىٰ وَٱلصَّـٰبِـِٔينَ مَنْ ءَامَنَ بِٱللَّهِ وَٱلْيَوْمِ ٱلْأَخِرِ وَعَمِلَ صَـٰلِحًا فَلَهُمْ أَجْرُهُمْ عِندَ رَبِّهِمْ وَلَا خَوْفٌ عَلَيْهِمْ وَلَا هُمْ يَحْزَنُونَ ۝

Surely, those who believe, and the Jews and the Christians and the Sabians, whoever have faith with true hearts in Allah and in the Last-day and do good deeds, their reward is with their Lord, and there shall be no fear for them nor any grief.

The Holy Qur'an, Surah Al-Baqara, Ayat 62.

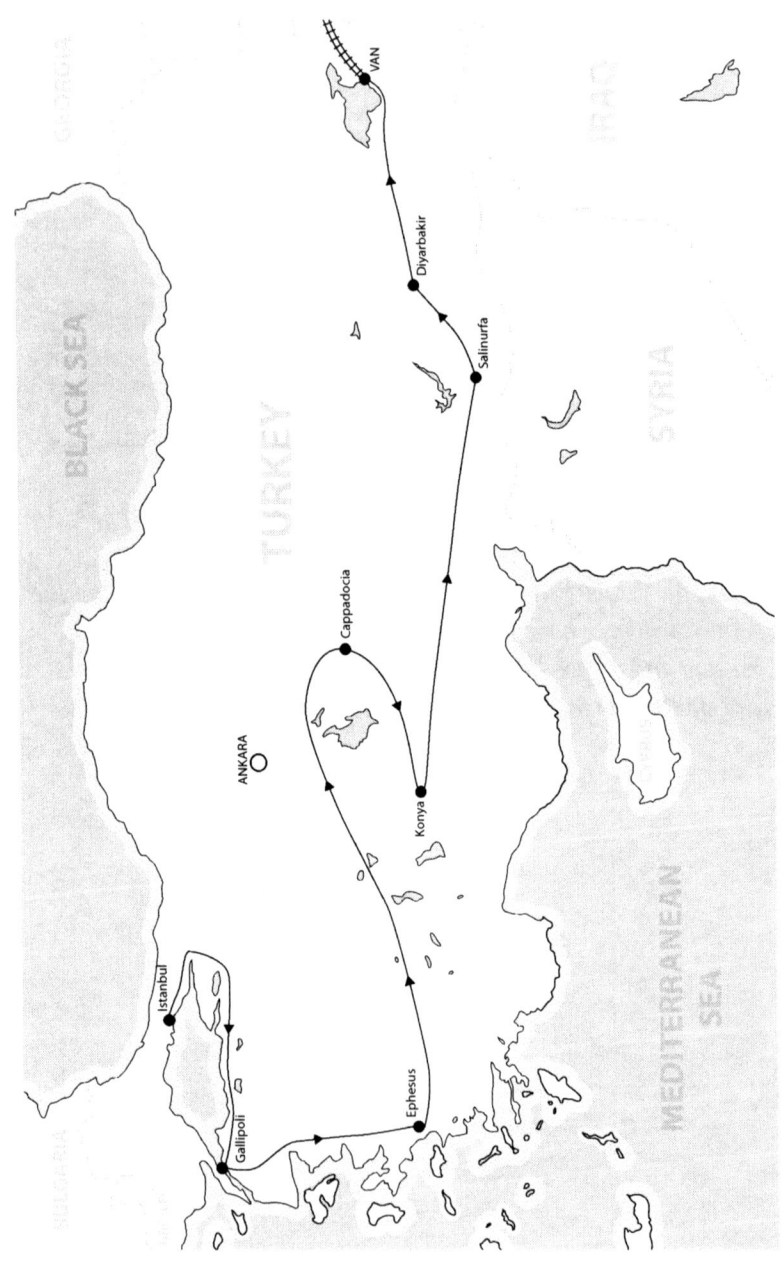

First steps: Istanbul - Van

Middle ground: Van - Salalah

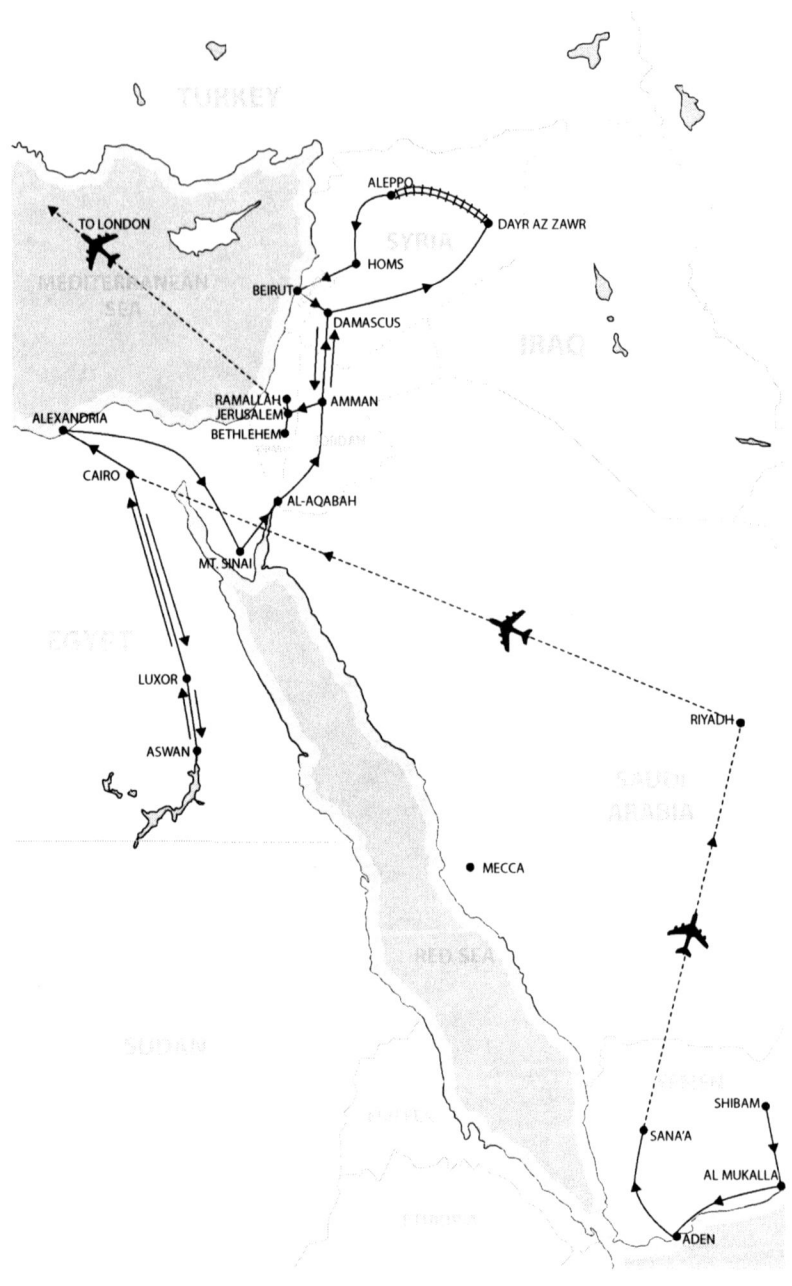

Home run: Al-Hawf - Jerusalem

Module 1:

Government and governance

The Animal Farm case study

Tehran, Iran
September 24

Since my arrival, the insidious nature of the Islamic republic and her government had grown more apparent as each day passed. Iran led my memory to recall the 'don't be a socialist now' GCSE literature schools are so apt at issuing, and the bleating of solid sheep 'four legs good, two legs *better*, four legs good, two legs *better*'. Despite the absence of overalls and slurry, Ayatollah Khomeini was Mr Jones.

Two religious bouncers stared at me with squinting, suspicious eyes. They stood arms folded, either side of a small door that lead into Ayatollah Khomeini's golden mausoleum. Their body language questioned my motivation in wishing to visit the shrine of the saviour of Iran, who in 1979 had led a popular wave of protest against the despotic and western sycophant shah, Reza Pahlavi.

The bouncers sported tasteless modern acrylic suits with

clergyman black dog-collars and a cheap zip in the place of cheated buttons. I walked towards the shrine's entrance before ostentatious bear paws struck out from the two flankers at the door. The charmless pair demanded my camera. I feared their shifts would end at a convenient time to coincide with my departure and ultimately that of my camera. I faked bravery, refused, and walked back to a little storeroom where a more servile man took my camera and handed me a raffle ticket. After a thorough and officious inspection, the two security tyrants reluctantly acknowledged that my ticket was, as the thousands of tickets before, valid.

I walked through a high-tech looking metal detector that failed to bleep, as it had not been turned on. I remember thinking at the time that it was unnecessary. But my time in Iran would shed light as to why there was a need for security and why there were so many unhappy citizens who might have wished to deface the revolutionary Imam's tomb. The bitterness of his legacy still dominated daily life.

I walked into the enormous, industrial complex the size of an aircraft hangar. Triangular metal tubes sprouted from above and below supporting gigantic air vents. From the rough, naked ceiling fell cheap, unendearing, 'bling' plastic chandeliers. The floor started with a marble periphery, but was later replaced by a more frugal finish of lacquered green onyx slabs. Occasional decorative pillars perforated the onyx stone, each one surrounded by a bookshelf overflowing with Qur'ans. Hundreds of blue and red prayer mats blanketed the green floor leading up to the Imam's resting place.

Khomeini lay in *jinah* (heaven) under a vast golden dome with stained glass rosy red windows. The scene was reminiscent of a culinary fly net covering a joint of beef. The shrine had been encompassed by a rectangular latticed golden box. A small coffin lay in the centre, protected by a green and golden inlaid threaded blanket. As a precaution for those who may have forgotten the identity of the resident below the green drape, a framed photograph of the Ayatollah's determined, and slightly grumpy, face had been propped up against his coffin.

The religious followers had formed a line, all staring up at the metal epitaph of mixed Farsi and Arabic Qur'anic inscriptions. Each man read out the words under a hushed voice, prayer beads sliding through the fingers of the right hand. A perspex plastic box behind the golden grill presented a 10 cm mouth allowing Iranians to poke rial notes towards charitable causes. A sea of 10,000 rial notes had piled up around the perimeter of the rectangular receptacle, acknowledgement to the congregation's generosity.

To the right of the tomb, hundreds of men and their sons sat cross-legged, attentively listening to a sermon from a smart, white turban-wearing mullah.

The mullah loudly inspired his congregation with a hectoring voice that vacillated in volume. I lingered behind them and listened out for anything I could comprehend. I could only understand one word. It was spoken with fervour and beckoned omnipotent nods from the crowd, '*Amerikeyz*'. Bored, I left.

In the subway, station commuters waited patiently for the scuttling Chinese built trains to arrive. Unlike London, the trains were comfortable and clean and lacked the respiratory restricting, condensed carriages that sardined you between a closing door and a builder's atrophying armpit, although London did allow anonymity and opportunities for a roving eye. Tehran was the reverse. The two sexes were divided at the door. The exclusively female carriages would blur past the platform in a shadow of black penguin-like forms.

As the underground ran northwards I imagined the city's teeming bazaar above. The previous day, I had seen a butcher grip a sheep under his bicep and mangle a knife away at its twitching neck. The animal gurgled desperately as the oesophagus was torn apart. Near luminous red throthy blood edged along the pavement and congealed, accumulating in the gutter.

Taxi charges were prohibitively high for tourists such as me who carried their entire material wealth in cash due to the lack of international ATMs. I was forced to navigate around the city's unconquerable bus system. At Hafte-Tir, I left the subway and burrowed up to daylight before boarding the cramped 102 bus. Like the subway, I was forced to stand on the designated male only area. The bus hissed off, away from the poor, smog-ridden south to the opulence of Tajrish square and the northern suburbs.

Staring out of the greasy hair-smeared windows, the foreign embassies seemed to battle for regional dominance. Their hundreds of metres of concrete walls and razor wire fences enclosed the diplomats in country estate-sized gardens. I jealously imagined the Foreign and Commonwealth Office employees sipping a plethora of *haraam* inebriants.

The American Embassy was not granted such luxury. The previous day I had walked 400 metres south of Hafte-Tir to find the now defunct embassy. The embassy had been renamed the 'US Den of Espionage' and stood empty, deprived of her rightful staff, whose last cohort had been barricaded in during the revolution of '79. The 'Muslim student followers of the Imam's line', a rag-tag brigade of students, then stormed the embassy and held the staff hostage for a symbolic 444 days.

Since 1979, the embassy's walls had acted as a propaganda

canvas for anti-American rhetoric. Much to my annoyance, the most fervent and abusive political painting and slogans had been euthanized with drab grey paint. The infamous image of bombs descending upon the letters 'U S A' with a grim reaper looking down from above with a sybaritic smile had been removed.

Yet, the pernicious notoriety of the United States had been visually maintained by murals and paintings around Tehran. The artists had depicted the US's international "PR failings" of more recent years. The events of Abu Ghraib decorated a billboard with hooded Iraqi prisoners wearing black Klu Klux Klan hoods as they looked to the ground, while a small figure of a Caucasian, and unforgivably female, soldier stood holding a rope leashed to her conical victims.

The 102 stopped at Tajrish Square where I ran and weaved my way between lanes of traffic that disregarded the safety of pedestrians. I retraced my steps from the morning back to an apartment block where my host, an Iranian businessman, lived. I walked self-consciously as teenage girls coming out of school laughed as I passed them.

Budhra sat looking bored in his armchair watching the factually biased state news channels that sabotaged the day's events. As with many Iranians of his age, he had witnessed the revolution and unlike his young progeny could compare the juxtaposed lives both before and after 1979. A Zoroastrian from birth, he had a mischievous face that hinted to his love of teasing people, usually as a means of convincing others of his opinions.

Before delving into our usual lengthy conversations, we both stared vacantly at the news, which like Tehran's many murals focussed on the evils of America.

A triumphant newscaster spoke exemplary English, smugly

announcing the defeat of American efforts to force Iran into nuclear co-operation at the United Nations. After a swift victory, we were then told of America's bombing campaign in northern Iraq, in which cross-border errors resulted in the death of many Turkish villagers. Next up, US forces in Iraq had cornered off an Iraqi town. Trade had come to a standstill affecting the lives of the innocent.

Middle Eastern objections to US influence in the region culminated in a video of Egyptians in Cairo burning the star-spangled flag before a meeting of the Arab League. The anchorman reassured us that revenge had been extracted as militia had bombed a US compound in Iraq. Finally, the news ended with an update on a US soldier who had been found guilty of abusing three naked Iraqi detainees.

Despite the fact that the actual events had occurred, it was depressing that the Iranian state news deliberately broadcast such savage and monotonous bias. But what was equally depressing was the sheer abundance of stories the agency was able to choose from.

It was my first experience of when the phrase 'the world is flat' rang true. The influence of quick and free-flowing media was evidently widening the gap between 'us' and 'them'.

Budhra was fed up and skipped through an abundance of Farsi opposition channels broadcast from America's West Coast or 'Tehrangeles'. Most of the channels were apolitical, filled with seraphic women prancing around to American-produced Farsi pop music. The picture quality rapidly deteriorated as grey specks crept into the resolution until we sat staring at a fuzzy screen.

'Bastards!' Budhra bellowed taking it personally. 'They've done it again! This happens every night. They're putting out static interference to stop me watching these foreign channels.'

Budhra edged forward, creaking out of his chair. He walked into the kitchen and started breaking ice into his glass before adding vodka, which like his satellite dish was wholly illegal. He slammed the fridge door to the objection of clinking bottles.

'Bloody Ministry of Information bastards are always trying to stop channels like the BBC and CNN.'

He slurped noisily from his glass and happily returned to his chair.

'So where have you been hiding all day?'

I dutifully told him of my visit to Ayatollah Khomeini's shrine. No action was ever half hearted with Budhra. He exploded.

'Why did you want to go and see that man's grave? What? You think that man is a hero?' I looked at him defensively. He continued.

'The old Shah kicked Khomeini out. Then once the Shah fled the country Khomeini returned telling the people that the Shah had stolen all their money and that he was an American stooge. Khomeini then proclaimed that the Shah had cheated the people out of the profits made from the exports of Iranian oil. Then guess what the bloody man did?'

I shrugged my shoulders.

'He proclaimed he'd go around to every household and give them some of this 'stolen' money.'

'So what happened?'

'Are you stupid Charlie?' He paused as though expecting an answer.

'Of course Khomeini couldn't do that and when he first arrived in Tehran he was shown on TV telling everyone how he would allow religious and political freedom, and that he wouldn't personally get involved in politics. But look at Iran now! Everyone knows that's rubbish. Khomeini called himself the 'Spiritual Leader' but he controlled bloody everything. You can guess *that* TV footage was never broadcast again.'

I could understand that unrealistic lucre promises by a religious leader were unlikely to materialise and engender such bitter outpourings as Budhra's. But I was unconvinced that a learned, Qom-trained, Shia *Mujtahid* theologian would intentionally lie and deceive those who rose to support him.

On hearing my doubts, Budhra looked at me in total dismay.

'Do you know how much money it costs to import foreign vehicles?' he snapped. I didn't understand the relevance of his question. He went on to explain.

'To import one foreign vehicle, you have to pay a mark up tax of 200% of the original price. Imagine that for a car? For one of those big American truck things. Anyone in Iran who can afford to import a vehicle like that has to be connected to the ruling families. All these people are in it to help themselves. They don't care about the nation. I'll give you an example. Let us imagine a minister in charge of building roads … public works. He'll look after his own. Maybe he'll give a contract to build some road to one of his cousins or brothers. He will ignore other companies who could do the same job for a cheaper price.'

Once allowed to roll, Budhra snowballed into a rightful tirade, and continued until he was confident we were both in agreement. He thought it a waste of my time to come to Tehran and leave having learnt nothing of the 'truth' as he put it.

Clambering from his seat he looked at his watch, raising an eyebrow in displeasure.

'We've got to stop chatting now. Layan's invited us to dinner tonight. We're going in half an hour,' he looked at me disapprovingly, 'and please wear a clean shirt.'

* * *

Budhra stood on the side of the road hailing a taxi back to Tajrish Square. The yellow cars zipped past each other in a manic scramble. It seemed that thorough and rigorous driving tests were not a priority of the Islamic republic. A pedestrian and a driver had to literally place their safe passage in the hands of Allah. Iran is still ranked number 1 in the global league table for the highest number of road-related fatalities and injuries. The crude figure is 38,000 per annum.

Before we arrived, I leant through to the front seat asking Budhra about the anti-American murals and paintings around the city. Budhra gave a cursory glance to the taxi driver, assessing the likelihood of him understanding English.

'Forget all that. It's just a farce. The Iranian people don't hate the Americans. But you see the government has to keep up the image of the evil 'imperialists' or the 'Great Satan' of the USA. That was the foundation of Khomeini's message and if they stop supporting this 'message', then the government fear that the people will lose confidence in the revolution and the Islamic state may be overthrown. For the government, it's all about keeping the status quo.'

Our taxi sped past Tajrish Square and continued travelling north before stopping outside a little bazaar that separated the main road from private houses. Walking through the bazaar little flags hung over the path blessing the martyrdom celebrations a few days earlier. The swishing flags recognised the deaths of over 300,0000 Iranians in the inconspicuous Iran–Iraq war of the 1980s. Budhra started to talk in a hushed voice about the war and his country's reliance on pre-revolutionary purchased American equipment. This logistical dependency later lead to the embarrassing *Iran-Contra Affair* in 1986.

'It's all bullshit. Even when Khomeini was still in charge, when Iran was fighting Iraq, the government was still doing business with the Israelis. The Israelis would buy parts for our American-made equipment from the US. Then they would sell them on to us. The Israelis made a great profit out of selling these spare parts at 10 times their original price. Yet, all the time Khomeini denounced the Jews and 'Zionist conspirators'.

Budhra had a love of aphorisms. 'One lesson you must learn Charlie: Politics has no principles'.

Budhra had sounded defamatory towards the Israelis which surprised me as he did not share his government's dogma on most issues. I asked him about his views on the commonly labelled 'Zionist aggressors'.

'I really loved Israel.' I stared at him taken aback. 'You have to go to Israel. I went to Tel Aviv for three weeks holiday, just before I started university at Cambridge. But I couldn't leave. I spent 3 months there. God, their women are beautiful!'

* * *

We arrived at Layan's stylish house. Plump cushioned chairs had been laid out in a manicured garden that centred around a spouting water fountain. Guests sat sipping aperitifs, chatting with great excitement about the arrival of an Iranian opposition leader from America. A 'Tehrangeles' channel had announced the doctor's pending arrival and his summoning of every Tehranian to come out on to the streets as a show of 'consolidation' against the current government.

Budhra was disappointingly softly spoken and charming that evening, as he sat at the opposite end of a long, regal table. I had been placed between a witty Iranian lady to my left and, as per the vulnerability of dinner parties, a noncommunicative, short, dumpy and balding man on my right. He made no attempt to mask his thoughts that there was nothing to be gained from talking to a boring British youth.

I chose to make his evasion difficult by doggedly engaging him in pedantic political speculation. Despite an unwillingness to converse, I had been told that he had experienced a great deal of political trauma during recent years. Realising the need to quickly subdue this gnat by his side he rushed through his story, explaining the events in a flash.

'When the revolution occurred in 1979, the Shah was overthrown and Iran became an Islamic republic headed by an Imam called Ayatollah Khomeini.' He spoke in a wonderfully patronising way. 'Everyone who had supported the old Shah was investigated. Those who had not already fled abroad were tortured or more often killed, depending on the severity of their supposed 'crime'. My family was accused of being associates and sympathisers of the old regime. Since that day we have had a terrible legal battle with the revolutionary courts to prove our innocence. However, a few years ago we lost the case. Men arrived at my house and seized everything we had. All our financial assets and bank accounts were frozen. I had no choice but to move quickly, so my family and I fled the country.'

I felt instant guilt for my callous insensitivity and my impertinent personal thoughts of the man. It was surprising that the legal and political persecution stemming from the revolution was still being pursued despite the passing of over two decades. With retrospective regret, I pushed him a little further, asking where his family were now. He looked angry at having the topic raised again. 'We are now in Paris, but please I don't want to talk about it!' With that he turned to his neighbour.

The tale of two Hosnis

Cairo, Egypt
March 8

Cairo had been awake for hours. Beeping car horns from the main road still pierced the tranquillity of the dusty square where trees hung lazily out over the ring road, their leaves quietly falling on to cars below. A virgin Mercedes had quickly lost her shiny newness with scratches and marks of Cairo's impatient drivers and the faecal offerings of song birds' carpet bombing from the branches above.

From my high vantage point, I could spy down on the couple of lazy square 'gardeners'. The two did not seem too interested in physically pursuing their vocation. Instead they sat, leaning up against their rickety wooden shed, admiring their creation of vegetable patches and small trees that girdled the thirsty yellow grass. The pair were a rare sight in such a cruel and competitive city. They seemed content, listening to Amr Diab pop ballads that warbled from a radio, their shesha smoke adding to the gaseous haze that compressed downwards in the city's chronic smog.

Two pugilistic beats at the door announced the late arrival of my tour guide, the loved, yet feared Hosni, the taxi driver-tour guide. His smart moustache greeted me with hirsute smiles and a friendly 'welcome, welcome to Egypt'. He was to be an individual among his class and failed to display the irksome characteristics of his taxi colleagues who were the masters of tourist trickery.

Outside, his chariot awaited, the ubiquitous black Cairo cab with an excessively squished snout and the more personal 'go fast' white stripes from bonnet to boot. Hosni welcomed me with true chauffeuresque charm, opening the passenger door that hung low on its dying hinge. The car's rusting body work flexed under the strain of the loose door. The engine reluctantly grunted into life and we pirouetted around at wheel-screeching speed and dived into the traffic. Wing mirrors remained deprived of even a cursory glance.

Hosni was keen to set out in a hedonistic frame of mind and lent over my lap to fish away at the glove compartment. His wily hand reappeared with thick paper rolled spliffs crumbling hashish that spilled out onto my lap. I felt an absurd guilt for not wishing to be an accomplice. There was a moment of disappointed silence. Hosni gently shrugged his shoulders, and recalled the happy memories of an Australian brother in arms who had once joined him in a hazy day, long gone.

He soon perked up and proudly reeled off all the names he could muster for cannabis. His hands interchanged from the wheel to floor in search of the elusive lighter. In momentary embarrassment he reassured me. 'but don't worry, Charlie. I have stopped smoking much … I have smoked too much before and it made me very ill. I didn't just smoke, I would take pills and drink alcohol all at once. It gave me a really bad stomach.' Sitting alongside the hash sat a thick pink bottle of medicine that Hosni slugged back intermittently to quell his acidic stomach.

We headed east across the Nile. To our north, the island of Zamalek breached the sky with the rooftops of the Marriot and the Sheraton. On the eastern bank, the old taxi shuddered up a rising road where adolescent conscript soldiers stood looking hot and irritated in riot gear. They made a long interwoven line of bodies that spread out in a challenging, impenetrable barricade along the pavement. Each man slung a Kalashnikov over one shoulder, and waved a baton in hand. Others clutched big riot shields. Their reinforcements waited still further to the rear, pushing cumbersome black bullet-proof doors on wheels. Behind the police, the beautiful Omar Makram mosque brimmed to its maximum peak capacity with Friday prayers and the Imam's sermon. Hosni secretly pointed to the soldier from within the taxi:

'Look! They are there to control the people praying inside the mosque. It is a Friday today, and the Imams always talk against the government and the president Hosni Mubarak. When he has finished, people will come outside and cause big fights.'

We continued up a raised bypass. The first white-robed Muslims were beginning to exit from Omar Makram's thick wooden doors. We were too early to see any potential scuffles as our taxi zoomed off down the cornice, hand-railing the pea green waters of the Nile, before heading further east in search of the cadaverous 'City of the Dead.'

We descended into an underpass before veering off down a narrow dirt track that funnelled past mud stucco walls, eventually opening up into a small car park. In front of us in a small square, sat old men patiently waiting beside a bubbling falafel stand. A cook mashed and rolled balls of chickpeas in his hands before placing them in a vat of hissing oil.

Opposite the lunch queue a **Bawab**, a doorman, sat on an uneven stool at the entrance to a small and dusty mosque. Seeing the two of us approach, he jumped to his feet and scurried to attention before supervising us wandering around the mosque's dark interior. Overhead, thick arches of white and red stone held up the dome, where dozens of song birds flew from one chandelier to another, liberally staining a prayer carpet with their offerings. Hosni crouched down on his haunches by the mihrab using the small Mecca aligned alcove to avoid the aerial bombardment. On his knees, he bent over, rubbed then kissed a cold black imprint of enormous size 15 feet.

'This is very holy. These are the footprints of Muhammad the prophet.' He wished to remain in prayer and left me to climb up the minaret staircase.

I soon understood Hosni's reluctance to join me. The stone staircase wound around with killingly steep steps. At the top of the minaret I had a bird's eye view outpost that looked down on the Dead City's irregular geography. My view stretched to the outer wall that demarcated an area previously reserved for the dead, and their subsurface rectangular tombs whose casing rose from the ground.

With immeasurable levels of rural migration to Cairo and a bulging population where one in three are under the age of 15, the deceased made way to provide accommodation for new, sacrilegious colonisers. Tomb slabs had been prised apart, the past occupants' peace disturbed by burrowing mortals. From my perch I could see recent modifications as foundations of old tombs had provided the bedrock for rising brick walls. Occasional heads would pop up from the depths of their underground lairs, pin pricks in a labyrinth of mud plaster and brick rubble.

Returning to the car, I asked Hosni who these residents were and why here, on the beds of the dead, did they choose to live?

'The people who live here originally came from the Suez after the Israelis invaded the area and pushed them all out. Cairo was already full and the government had nowhere to put the 250,000 people. They had nowhere else to go.'

* * *

'Ahhh! Why do they always have to do this? It's robbery'. I sat quietly in the back of a car as two Egyptian friends negotiated the difficult task of parking in Cairo. Sharifah smiled sardonically and waved a *shukran* to illegal ticket attendants. It was a tragic reflection of an uncontrolled demographic eruption and a stagnant economy that unemployed men made a profession of claiming public streets to be private with the aim of extracting a charge for parking. Sharifah continued in her rage: 'you do anything in Cairo and there is someone there, waiting to demand **baksheesh**, for doing nothing.'

Ahmed her husband found her outburst amusing, his face shining with a childish smile the more Sharifah spoke.

'Calm down baby. This is only because we've got Strawberry Cheeks (my new nickname due to my rosy Caucasoid complexion) with us.' He guffawed in laughter as we edged out from the pavement on to the 26th July road. Our car raced through the afternoon traffic, across the hot tarmac-smelling roads to Zamalek where the young and wealthy remained cocooned from the *fellaheen* peasants.

Sharifah rummaged through the back seat looking for one of Ahmed's particular Trance CDs. Jumping beats shot through the car as Ahmed always levelled the rear speakers to the maximum. I was interested to see what the rich thought of their government, as the resulting privations of the masses would never directly affect them. I leant forward to shout over the dull speaker thuds.

'What government?' Sharifah replied looking in the rear view mirror. 'The only person who controls Egypt is Hosni Mubarak. The ministers are not really elected. They're all a bunch of crooks supporting the president. Everyone is too scared to challenge the bastard.'

'What do you mean they are too scared?', came my wheedling reply.

'*Hallas*, if anyone tries to oppose Mubarak they'll have serious problems. At first, you're threatened and then some convenient 'accident' happens. People die in these 'accidents'.

There was a pause, everyone returned to their own thoughts. We stopped outside their flat. Sharifah turned her head to face me on the back seat.

'Hosni Mubarak is clever. He knows that all he has to do is please the Americans. After that, he can do whatever he likes in Egypt. Right now he is training his son to take over as president. You can look anywhere in this country, Charlie.' Her hands flailed in anger, 'and people are always so poor. There are no jobs and no houses. People cannot even afford to buy their children books and pens for school, and that's if they can afford to allow them to go to school. She looked exhausted by the city's draining character and the futility of her words.

'You have to understand. It is no wonder people are becoming extremists. Many people would prefer the Muslim

Brotherhood to Mubarak.'

* * *

The next month, two separate bomb blasts detonated in Cairo, another exploded six months later in the tourist enclave of Sharm Al Sheikh. There have been many more since then.

On 11th February this year Hosni Mubarak finally resigned after nationawide mass protest. In Tahrir Square one protestor's placard read, '***Mubarak Ya-kul Quloob Ar-Rijal'*** - 'Mubarak, he eats the hearts of men'.

Thieves of democracy

Aden, Yemen
December 3

Lifting my camera to focus, I tried to catch the British colonial character Aden's 'At-Tawahi' district still possessed. The warehouses resembled Plymouth docklands, the masonry of semi-circle black arches of Aden basalt, neatly curved like a birthday cake, with white cement icing topping off the delicatessen illusion. The coastal air carried a heavy saline taste, the salt tainting the resolute wooden doors. Shared taxis zipped across the waterfront, where thousands of lights glittered off gargantuan oil tankers lying in the port.

At-Tawahi's charm also extended underfoot, as the cobbled streets of fist-sized smooth stones gave the area a London mews-like quality, though the district's beauty could only be attributed to the United Nations, who had poured in money where the Yemeni government could not. The street lamps cast a spooky orange glow, shimmering on the warehouses' broken glass windows that hid deserted rooms within.

Quite silently two men tiptoed up behind me, creeping from the Crescent Hotel's car park. They encircled me. Each man stood either side of me with querying faces. I braced myself to be mugged. The fatter of the two looked over his thick beard and pointed his index finger in a 'wait here' gesture. I looked back. Confused, I stupidly obeyed. I watched the silhouette of their bulky frames disappear down the dark alley from which they came.

Transport arrived in perfect timing. Henry, a young British expatriate working in the oil refinery, beeped his blue Toyota in greeting. He stopped and I explained the strange encounter.

'Oh,' said Henry 'you took a picture of the warehouses here?'

'Yes, is that a crime?'

'Quite possibly,' he replied.

The two men came back. Familiarity spread across the faces of all. The chubby one greeted Henry with a Neanderthal handshake and guttural Arabic sounds. I waited in silence as all three conversed.

'Right. Just get in the car now!' Henry quickly ordered.

Without protesting, I climbed into the passenger seat. The two Yemeni's stayed on the street corner, waving as we went. Henry waited to speak until we were out of sight.

'Those two men were from the Yemeni secret police. They said you were alone, taking pictures of those warehouses.'

I was confused by now. 'What was wrong with that?' I asked.

'Don't worry, you weren't to know, but they torture people inside those derelict buildings. As you can imagine, it's a bit of a sensitive site. It is not a problem. I knew one of the men, the chubbier one. His brother was stabbed in the leg in a nightclub last year. The doctors here said he would lose his leg if he didn't have specialist treatment, so I got some people together and we raised the money and flew him to Dubai for the operation.'

It was one of many quiet Christian acts Henry had done in the area. During my time in Aden I met many Yemenis who casually approached his car for a familiar chat. There were many people he had helped, and there were few who did not know of his kindness. The Yemenis of Aden had named him *'Anza Al-Jibal'*, 'The Mountain Goat' on account of his daily runs on the south-western foot of Jebel Shamsan.

Every afternoon he would park his car, overlooking Conquest Bay. Couples strolled hand in hand along the beach, men staring into the eyes of their women, the only outwardly visible sign of the personality behind the black wall of the *niqab*. The setting sun cast a blinding yellow reflection off the sea. The Jebel radiated soft red earthy colours as shadows etched across, shading the rock face.

Usually the two of us ran in tandem, although sometimes Henry's young Western-educated Yemeni friend, Anwar, joined us. Our merry group of three yomped up and along the mountain ridges. Amused faces turned to watch the sweating spectacle, failing to understand why anyone would chose to voluntarily run. Henry lived up to his nickname, displaying his great agility with quick calculative steps as he dish-dashed like a ballerina over the loose stones.

A family of feral dogs gave a terrifying rabies-inspired chase. We found refuge hidden away in a small cove where a *dhow* had been moored, hemmed in by the cliffs. Her beautifully crafted bow pointed out to the Western edges of Somalia.

After scraping our knees on the loose rock scree, the

evening sunset would descend as we lay on our backs in the water suspended by the rocking waves of the Gulf of Aden.

Three metres from the water's edge sat the rusting hull of a small landing craft, a mark of the civil war when rebels tried to capture the bay.

The previous month in Yemen turned out to be the most interesting and enjoyable of the entire odyssey. I was humbled by the famous old-fashioned Arab manners I had read about, and subsequently experienced among the poorest of people, in the poorest country in the Middle East. Here, in rural areas, farmers would club together, and unbeknown to me, would pay my bus fares, before walking off, asking and expecting not an ounce of gratitude. The Yemenis I had met so far possessed a baffling appreciation for tourists who wished to visit their country. They had viewed me as a guest, and therefore, in their mind it was the responsibility of all to see to my comfort and happiness. The people were charming, yet security was paramount to the point of annoyance. Yemen was gloriously unpredictable and had maintained an enigmatic image of frankincense, Baobab trees and demonic tourist-abducting tribesmen. Due to a lack of Arabic, I had not been able to converse with Yemenis about their countrymen.

I took the opportunity during one of our afternoon Jebel runs to ask Anwar to explain to me the juxtaposition between the hospitable Yemenis I had met and the hype of Al-Qaeda-related tribesmen.

'Oh, it's the government that indirectly causes these kidnappings. As all governments do, taxes are collected. But here in Yemen, the government doesn't re-distribute the money. Of course it is far easier for the president Abdullah Saleh, to call these kidnappers 'terrorists' when really they are ordinary people. They don't hate Westerners. They only take hostages to pressurize the Yemeni government to provide schools, hospitals and good roads. Beyond Sana'a everyone is ignored.'

I had heard that irrespective of schools and roads, tribal leaders expected the government to pay them a dividend each year, and felt cheated of their rights when this was not the case. Whilst corruption in the Middle East was as common as camels, it still seemed a difficult justification to hold Westerners as intermediaries. Anwar seemed to ignore my final point and objected to my complacency on corruption.

He shook his head in definite disagreement, 'No. How can corruption ever be acceptable? Such evil, in a nation as poor as Yemen. Arabs prefer one good and fair Sheikh to many thieves.'

A nation's desire for democracy?

Sana'a, Yemen
December 9

'Be careful that man is trying to cheat you,' I was warned.

'That man', was a shop keeper who weaved around his clothes shop with shifting eyes, searching for clues as to which leather motorbike jacket I fancied. The cautioning voice came from another customer standing by a rack of thick winter coats. Next to him, his diminutive friend was trying on garments. After his exhortation a bitter argument ensued. The Arabic language's abrupt caesuras and cutting, raspy words created a tempestuous display.

'Let us go now. This man is very angry.' The taller of my two advisers warned me.

Together we retreated at pace down the small cobbled streets. Happier shouts and laughter echoed from children, playing across the streets. Others leant out of thick white plastered window frames. We clashed with bands of stray cats who patrolled the old city in feline turf wars.

'I am sorry, he was not a good man,' my new friend continued. 'May I introduce myself? I am Ali and this is my friend Hamik, and that man ...' Ali waved his hand in the rough direction of whence we had come, '... was very angry with me because I told you that he was trying to cheat you. After that we thought it best to leave.' Hamik leant forward, the shorter of the two. We shook hands.

'So Hamik! It is an honour of ours to have a foreigner in our company. Tell me. Are you hungry?' I did not have time to reply before Ali opened the door of a Suzuki minivan proudly beckoning me in: 'Please this is my taxi. We will go to a restaurant I know down this street.'

The two turned out to be old friends who had both trained as medical doctors in Romania in their youth, and as such, had an air of arrogance and were disparaging about their countrymen who they viewed as lethargic and apathetic in their attempts to better their lives. Despite being qualified doctors, Ali and Hakim were good examples of the Yemen's decrepit public services. As Ali explained,

'But we are not doctors now. We are in business.' He laughed in irony. 'We need to make money and saving lives doesn't make money.'

Ali's driver drove us to the restaurant down Ali Abdul Mogni Street, past pedestrians who ambled along the pavement comparing the numerous milkshake cafés and mobile phone shops. Lonesome men stooped over unfurled blankets displaying Kalashnikov accessories of extra bayonets, straps, magazines and pistol grips. A shabby army personnel carrier blocked off the entrance to a smart, modern bank. I pointed to it in surprise. Ali responded in a matter of fact way,

'There is no need to worry. The police and the army are all

out on the streets at the moment. Someone or some group has threatened an attack, so the authorities must be careful.' Ali let out a short, patronizing laugh, with the words, 'This is not London.'

Ali spoke quickly to his driver prior to the minivan making an abrupt U-turn in the middle of the road. Oncoming traffic honked in protest as we skidded to a halt on the other side of the road outside a busy fish restaurant. Red, yellow and orange plastic ropes containing hundreds of small twinkling lights irradiated the opposing shops like a budget theme park.

'It is such a privilege to have you here. It is not often we can have a foreigner to come and eat with us. We usually have to do with these Yemenis.' Ali spat the words out in a comic display, yet his voice resonated with disgust and a sense of distinction between himself and 'the Yemenis'. He sensed my noncompliance.

'I am sorry, I will explain it for you. You see in Yemen, many people like to criticise Britain and especially America for the way they behave. I do not mean that most Yemenis have such extreme views as Osama Bin Laden, but you must understand this: most Yemenis criticise the Western life. Many say the Americans are too fat, that they love drugs and have too much sex with women.'

'And you hate that as well, Ali?' I replied.

'It doesn't matter what I think about these things. Of course, some of them are bad, but the people here, they do not know how strong America is. Americans are proud to be American. They love their country. But here in Yemen, a man will only think about himself. He wants his food, his cigarettes and his Qat. Yemeni men cause too much trouble starting fights and tribal feuds. Do you understand what I mean?'

I nodded, he continued:

'And you know why?' I shook my head. My mind leapt back to lessons on political theory as Ali answered his question, revealing an unwitting agreement between the average Yemeni and the social-political theorist Isaiah Berlin: that liberty was an inadequate answer to social inequality.

'Some Yemenis behave in this way because they simply have nothing to lose. Even if we wanted to have a real democracy, which I think is the best way to run a country, it would be quite impossible, *hallas*, it could never work. People are too selfish and too poor. People need to learn that if they work hard they will have something to gain. However, in Yemen no one wants to improve themselves.'

Drinking with soldiers: A toast to freedom?

Jerusalem, Israel and the Palestinian territories
March 2

Israeli border agents at the King Hussein crossing soon found my second passport and the array of unwanted visas from far off enemies including Iran, Yemen, Saudi Arabia, Syria and Lebanon. My two British passports were no longer my property as a wave of commotion ensued. A macabre figure appeared in latex gloves and demanded I appear before him in boxer shorts for a body search. He seemed disappointed not to find any incriminating needles or narcotics.

After a thorough x-ray scanning, the contents of my bag were laid out before us and a tall young guard as I was held to account for each object like an inventory between a slothful tenant and his neurotic landlord. Each contact on my phone was checked and I endured a 3 hour wait while my mobile phone was meticulously scrutinised. Every 'Ahmed' and 'Mohammed' contact in the Nokia would invite a series of questions: Who was he? Where did you meet him? What is your relationship with him? The last question seemed to imply all sorts of licentious associations, as though I were a sexual deviant on a tawdry tour of the Arab world.

'Hey! You're looking nervous. Why? Have you got something to hide?'

I didn't, but the Israeli border agency possessed a unique ability to make one feel guilty, regardless of innocence. An immigration colleague soon joined the two of us. I sat, both men stood demanding questions. My attempts at amused, amicable smiles were not returned by my masters, who played the dichotomy of the interrogator and his mute during my trial.

'I just don't understand. Why did you go to all these countries? You should be sunbathing on a beach in Goa.'

The jury simply failed to understand any desire to venture into these poor, dangerous and predominantly Muslim lands. Instead, young Israelis finished their often traumatic military conscription and usually left the bad lands of the Middle East, clutching a sticker-smeared acoustic guitar for a party pilgrimage to India and Southeast Asia. The beaches of Goa and Phuket were permissible destinations, not Tehran and Damascus.

I sat from midday until 9 that night. The same lanky guard reappeared and pointed me back towards Jordan. 'Come back tomorrow at 9.' He smiled knowingly. 'If you want to?'

The next day I paid my second instalment of Jordanian exit duty and crossed the small bridge over the thin river Jordan to my old friends. In case I had concealed any Semtex or still worse, a Qur'an, the same body and bag disembowelling began all over again.

It all felt a little James Bondish when I was informed that two 'special investigators' had arrived to see me. I was led away like a tethered donkey to a small portacabin where I hoped I would meet Mossad agents that would provide for heroic, sleuth stories back in the UK. Two men sat facing the door behind a small desk. Folders in hand, one was a short, round old man with a tall 20 something more Semitic-looking colleague. Much to my immature desire to be a victim, I was to be treated like an adult as they politely welcomed me and offered coffee.

The humpy-dumpty figure started a series of questions aimed at unwrapping my character and social-economic standing. 'Who is your father? What is his job? How much money do you have on you?' Next came the theological. 'Are you a Christian or have you converted to Islam? … No? … Are you thinking of converting?' I stated my C of E preferences which were all scribbled on paper obscured from my eyes.

I now needed to justify the purpose of my visit to Israel before I was bequeathed the right. We slowly worked through a list of names I had accumulated of people to meet. What were my reasons for visiting each and what connections were there? Did I have any Palestinian associations? 'Do you know anyone in Gaza? … No, then in the West Bank?' I truthfully pleaded innocent of any affiliation.

Once reassured, their questions stopped. The younger official waited with me in the portacabin while his senior disappeared. I felt a little more confident and asked him which department he belonged to and his ethnic origin. Unoffended by my impertinence, he openly told me he was in Israeli Special Forces. Nodding earnestly, I tried to sound an authority on Bravo 2 Zero and all things SAS. More interestingly, he told me of his father's decision to leave the Yemeni capital Sana'a for Israel at the end of the 1940s. I thought it could have been another topic of mutual interest.

'Why would I ever want to go there?', he said. I had tried a little too hard in ebulliently listing the places I had been to in Yemen and the wonders of the people. He looked at me with ridicule.

'No, It is so dirty and the people ... eh!'

A little after midday I was granted leave and negotiated a lift with a taxi driver to the nearest bus stop for Jerusalem. The driver wanted too many of my precious shekels. I stopped a guard who could have been no older than me and asked for the normal rate. He looked me up and down with the supercilious reply:

'Pay him half that amount, but I am not surprised he tried. You're a foreigner and you look naive, but, no offence. You just do.'

A five minute drive for the equivalent of ten pounds sterling took me to the edges of a small town where 18-year-old soldiers from the Israeli Defence Force (IDF) stood under a yellow bus shelter chatting amongst themselves, M16 American rifles or the smaller Colt carbines casually hung from their shoulders. Girls pouted, fighting for individuality with long pink nails and garish jewellery under their industrially issued uniforms, 9 mm Uzis swinging loosely by their sides. These teenagers looked more interested in eloping than fighting. It was clear why full moon beach parties and laced *bhang lassi* were of greater interest than the Holy Land. Men suffered three years of compulsory military service, for women a more lenient two. Ironically, if you were an ultra-orthodox *Haredi* Jew you were exempt from conscription.

Our bus wound along the Jordan Rift Valley hugging the Jordan River. The view of the valley's golden tranquillity contrasted with the more realistic images of twisting barbed wire and machine gun mounted 4×4s. Occasional white signs warned of land mines buffeting the two states. The bus often stopped for the young soldiers to decamp at numerous military bases that ran defensively along the border.

* * *

Jerusalem, Muslim Quarter

The olive green uniforms of an IDF foot patrol discreetly blended into the darkness past shut up souvenir shops along David Street, a VHF aerial swayed in the air revealing their position. Their dull rubber boots patted upon the cobbled streets.

I had stayed at a small hostel in the Muslim quarter of the old city where an amalgamation of students from all continents had converged. Our small band of four formed hastily constructed friendships as a spritely Colombian, Ricardo, led us through the old city along a well practised short cut to Jaffa gate via the Church of the Holy Sepulchre. Outside the city walls we passed a fellow itinerant backpacker who economically slept in his sleeping bag on a small patch of grass. The two Dutch members of our quartet debated how many hours of sleep he would get before being rounded up by a dispirited IDF patrol.

New Jerusalem was like any other modern city in many respects. The young filled bars and restaurants that ran all the way up Jaffa Road to Zion Square. But I had been warned by a former British Ambassador to Israel prior to my travels, not to be misled by the beauty and calm of the city. 'Always remember that you are in a fluctuating war zone. If you see a crowd of people running, don't stick around, just run'.

I had been similarly advised a second time by a pugnacious Jewish New Yorker who also deplored my ignorance in not knowing that Jerusalem was officially the capital of Israel (this was despite foreign embassies remaining in Tel Aviv in disagreement).

Remembering both lessons, we entered a dark 'Irish pub', one of those artificial, plastic 'pubs' that have spawned globally with inanimate leprechauns and an overstocked aviary of Guinness pelicans proliferating the walls.

The four of us sat in a dank corner as conspicuous tourists exchanging light travel stories comparing Levantine cities. I soon fell into a more biting conversation with a chubby, dark-haired Israeli girl on the next table. I was surprised, due to perceived physical restraints, to hear her announce that she was also a soldier on national service. 'We are all soldiers' she said, waving her hand to two men across the table. They looked at me with apprehensive nods.

After a few minutes, she invited me to join them. 'My friends are in the parachute divisions, and I am trained in logistics, sorting out supplies and provisions,' she continued, before embarking on a watered down version of her distant colleagues' border inquisition. Where was I from? What was I doing in Israel?

I was surprised when she seemed interested to listen to the trivialities of my ventures in the wilds of Iran and Yemen. She possessed an openness I had not yet seen in Israel. Of the few that I had met, I had found the Israelis sharp, forward and often cold, yet without the humour that could collectivise such characteristics under the banner of 'confidence'. I found this acutely among the young guards at the border, where for the first time during my Middle Eastern tour I could not extract any advantages from what I perceived to be a well-mannered tone of appeasement. The guards had increasingly mistrusted my best attempts at a calm, queue-abiding, English temperament the longer they were exposed to it.

I wrongly thought that due to the multinational nature of Israel's immigrant lineage, she would house a more receptive people. A barrier of disinterest and wariness seemed to divide the mostly religious grockles from the locals. Alcohol dissolved my aversions and I diplomatically shared these thoughts with her.

'I don't know if I agree entirely, but you're right in a way. We are very suspicious of any foreigners. We just don't understand why people would want to come to Israel and for this reason we don't talk to you foreigners'.

'Why are you talking to me then?' came my quick response.

She laughed to herself and raised her glass in the air, 'there are always exceptions.'

We became more serious and distant as I told her of my day trip to Bethlehem. The town was more warlike than ecumenical. On the outskirts, an Israeli bunker housed reluctant teenage soldiers who checked passports and ID cards to allow their prisoners to pass through a blank area of no man's land, before hitting the hugely controversial 30ft concrete slab wall that encircled the town. I had been warned by an angry Israeli man not to refer to the construction as a 'wall', but to use the less permanent noun, a 'fence' due to its ability to be deconstructed and removed in a number of large fragments. Peering through the walled entrance to the city, the roads were eerily empty like a ghost town. Few vehicles broke the wall's restrictions and ventured into the occupied West Bank without an elusive security pass. I arrived at a desperate scene of swarming taxi drivers, pushing amongst each other, begging me to take their car. The few shops that remained open, displayed a variety of dusty ornaments of the Virgin Mary cradling a baby Jesus. Tourism, the town's bread and butter, had declined in recent years, whilst irrespective of the 'fence' or 'wall' appellation, agriculture had been devastated by farmers being cut off from their fields. Factories had closed and the cost of living had rocketed, as supplies were quite literally 'imported' from outside the town.

Again my new friend sat attentively, listening to my version of the age-old conflict. I heroically concluded.

'If people are put in a situation with no real way of making money and are locked up as prisoners in their own towns, then how can Israel ever achieve peace? The 'fences' work only to enrage people, making their lives so utterly hopeless they might as well become suicide bombers. There seems little to lose.'

The pretty face shifted to scrunched eyes with a shaking head. Our amicable exchange was lost. She stared me down with fixed eyes.

'What do you know of achieving peace? You say those Palestinians have no freedom. Look where you are. You're in Jerusalem. We've lost count of how many buses have been destroyed by suicide bombings. You think Israelis have freedom? Everyday we live our lives in fear. We can't even take a bus without the risk of being killed. I know because I too was nearly killed by one of these suicide bombers. He got on the same bus but two stops after me. You think that man wanted peace?'

I tried to steer the argument back to the route of the suicide bomber's despair and the reasons for the futility of his life.

'What? Why do you people always think it's the Israelis' fault? Is it our fault the Palestinians have no strong leaders?

Fatah can't control these terrorist groups. We have to do it for them. What hope does Abbas have of leading these people?'

We moved away from the modern complexities of the Arab–Israeli argument as she sought sanctuary in the shell of Jewish identity and epochal territorial claims.

'The country 'Palestine' didn't exist until after the First World War. The Jews have kept their identity and attachment to this land for thousands of years. The Jews were pushed out against their will. Even before Judaism came into existence we have been a persecuted group. Our entire history is one of hardship … and the Holocaust. Do you not think we deserve a homeland?'

Her words tugged my memory of the girl with the red coat in 'Schindler's List' and Itzhak Perlman's masterful violin overlays. I could not sit with her and repudiate the events of the Second World War, though within that sadness lay layers of frustration and bitterness that the lessons and suffering of the Warsaw ghettos had not imprinted an abiding mark on history.

I could only think of the hurried graffiti I had seen that day sprayed upon Bethlehem's 'fence':

WARSAW 1940
BETHLEHEM 2005

The Cedar Revolution

Beirut, Lebanon
April 19

'You're lucky to be in Lebanon right now. It's all happening. Things are starting to change.' Juliet, the public relations officer at America's Beirut embassy had become the victim of 'the friend of a friend' circuit. Taking another sip from her water bottle, she looked exhausted from the afternoon's painful 'workout' in the embassy's air-conditioned gym. Beyond the balcony and confinements of the embassy, the Mediterranean peacefully rolled on, a condition Lebanon herself wished to emulate. But on Monday February 14, 2005, Lebanon had grasped the world's attention, as their Prime Minister Rafiq Al-Hariri was assassinated by a 1000-kg TNT car bomb. It was a death that rocked the country and the region in such a way few could have foreseen.

Lebanon was wounded by Hariri's death, although his legacy was interwoven within the very heart of the nation. He had taken a ravaged post civil war Lebanon and, using his own money as a starting point, rebuilt the place physically and politically, only to be cruelly murdered. Some eyes pointed accusingly at Israel, although despite previous Israeli iniquities, the majority of Lebanon looked East to Damascus.

With his death came a movement's birth, as the people of Beirut, a previously fractured city of a sanguinely divided society, congregated in downtown's barren Place De Martyrs. On the announcement of Hariri's death, the city united, bringing together past enemies to an extent never seen before.

Students had constructed a tented hamlet around the Place De Martyrs, a square dominated by a four-figured metal statue that has been an only too appropriate metaphor for the country's recent history. It is a bronze statue of a woman, leading three others and grasping a burning torch, her other arm free, pulling a man kneeling at her feet. The figure of the kneeling man had had his lower arm blown off by shrapnel during the civil war. The metal is now crinkled above his elbow and chest. Another figure had suffered the most with a hollow chest of perforated ribs as 7.62 mm small arms fire had mottled their previously smooth metal bodies. Behind a bench of marmoreal stone that encased the four, not a patch of grass remained exposed in the surrounding embankment. Tents ranging from military, 10 man monsters to two man Toblerones flapped in the light breezes.

On morning forays downtown, I would walk around the small tented community watching the students chat, whilst their leader, Hariri, smiled from huge boards suspended on stray tent poles. Inside the larger tents, the students had built generator-powered kitchens with a conventional armory of modern appliances. Red stickers pasted the area, with the words:

'Independence '05'

It was the logo of their movement. Glastonbury met Beirut with a political twist. A well-rigged stage had been erected, with shiny stage lights and huge box-like loudspeakers. The shiny bench encasing the four statues had been a platform for expression. Permanent black marker pens had spidered graffitied thoughts. A competition of messages to their last leader conveyed personal thoughts and subsequent aims.

'Farewell, dear Hariri, you were a man of honour in life and in death, you are a martyr ... they took your body away but your spirit lives on in our hearts' (from Rawan and Jana).

Lebanon's francophile influence continued with:

'Tous unis pour le Liban.'

It was encouraging to see schoolboy humour in reference to Lebanon's previously pro-Syrian president:

'Lahoud, pull out, my arse hurts!'

It was an exciting time. Hariri's death marked the end of Lebanese tolerance for self-seeking Syrian influence within her borders. The students before me wished for free elections and a government with an exclusive Lebanese voice. But it was not only the Syrians who conjured up such vehement opposition. The Lebanese had long held a deep resentment for any nation who tried to influence their country. This was evident in the people I met, who spoke of the civil war as a platform for the grievances of others, aired on Lebanon's fields.

Hariri was everywhere; his largest legacy to Beirut rose up from across the road from within the tented hamlet. His gift to his nation had been a beautiful, beige-sandy mosque. The exquisite carvings and patterns were just small examples of the generous budget Hariri set aside during the mosque's construction. The mosque was an example of incredible modern craftsmanship in masonry with weaving floral and calligraphied designs. Massive cranes towered over the mosque, bolted to the minarets for stability. The same cranes which, immediately after Hariri's death, were scaled by a harness-free madman who then crawled all the way to the ends to drape his small Lebanese flags.

Apart from the tented hamlet, 'Independence '05' had mounted a photo exhibition next to Hariri's and the six other assassinated men, who lay beside him in a marquee by the president's mosque. The exhibition showed photos of the Place des Martyrs immediately after the assassination. The square was filled with a sea of tiny heads that popped up like a bun of sewing needles. The tearful crowd waved the national flag and clutched pictures of their leader and the deceased entourage. There were even photographs of the bombsite. Dumbfounded people and policemen staggered around amongst a backdrop of upturned smouldering cars. Earlier photos showed a smiling Hariri during the final hours before his death, joking with other MPs, then waving to the public outside parliament, by the car that would ultimately be his coffin. Someone had scribbled on one of the plastic photos a synopsis of what they thought Lebanon stood for:

Liberty
Eager
Blessed
Anxious
Never resting
Overwhelmed
Nothing but *everything*.

Hariri's temporary mausoleum presented him as a nine-foot

giant. Enormous wreaths and five-foot profile pictures walled the coffin. A small hill of fresh flowers sat on top with flickering candles. Metal railings enclosed the immediate area while security guards allowed mourners to enter to pay their personal respects. A school boy had crafted an all too realistic model of the scene of Hariri's assassination on a little table. Cereal boxes had been used for buildings with Lego palm trees and battered and burnt Matchbox toy cars.

A separate photo exhibition displayed old pictures of Beirut during the civil war. The streets filled with defunct cars, strewn rubbish and giraffe-tall grass, clear indications of no man's land and sniper alleys. Once wild and feral, the city had turned itself around, but at what price?

Tucked away from the main spectacle was a small wing of more graves. In raised coffins lay the bodies of the seven other men who had died in the immediate blast, although more coffins were still required. Before I left Lebanon another man died after weeks of agonizing suffering. Each coffin lay covered in flowers. In place of a headstone, pictures of each man were positioned against the blue background of Hariri's stern face. The sixth tomb in the line had the youthful picture of a serious looking young man, close to my age in his early twenties.

* * *

St Joseph University, Rue Monot, Central Beirut

As I looked through the rose-tinted, bullet-proof windows, students sat with their knees tucked up on the university steps chatting together. The cumbersome embassy Chevrolet engine roared loudly as a bodyguard circled the car, before opening the rear passenger doors to let us out. Apart from appearing on Lebanese television during my stay, this was to be the only other major public appearance Juliet made during my time in Lebanon. On the top floor of St Joseph's Political Science wing, students continued to arrive, filling the large classroom which did not contain enough seats. Soon the walls were lined with young men and women.

During the next hour, I was to hear a cross-section of opinions from Lebanon's youth, an eager generation, who largely hoped to take their country into a democratic, truly 'Lebanese' future.

On a meagerly elevated stage, the president of the student's union appeared preoccupied with brushing back his well-crafted hair and inspecting his smart suit, before strutting his stately persona before us. My perception of him was not shared as everyone clapped when he stood to talk, chanting him on for a second term in office.

As Juliet rose to speak, the ambiance shifted as the crowd lacked the same conviviality. Not a soul clasped hands in applause. Yet here was a crowded room of undergraduates who had come to question Juliet, who in their eyes, represented America and to question her role at this opportune time.

Juliet stood eyebrows raised in anticipation of the first question. As is often the case, few wanted to break the ice. After a tense wait all eyes shifted to a gutsy man who jumped to the heart of the debate. Without charm, he asked what others feared to ask. 'What kind of American 'freedom' was the torture of Iraqis in Abu Ghraib, and why do you patronize the Arabs about this freedom?' Despite the personal implication, Juliet did not pause for thought.

'This is 2005. A lot has changed in the world. What are US interests in 2005 you ask?' The students looked at her blankly.

'September 11th brought about a profound shift in the way

Americans saw the Middle East. Before, we compromised stability for oppressive regimes. We learnt that, by ignoring this, anger grew within the Middle East against the US. All people must believe in a future. Now the US is holding the leaders of nations accountable to meet our standards of democracy and the basic rights of empowerment. We want to see the greatest number of opportunities reaching ordinary people.'

The audience looked unconvinced, though she had not finished:

'Look at Lebanon!' She paused for impact. 'You can't have a truly democratic state with another country dominating. When Hariri died, you, the people of Lebanon said 'Enough', and we, the Americans, are trying to respond to that.' She thrust her hands forward to the crowd conjuring enthusiasm.

'It's an exciting time in Lebanon. People are saying they aren't content, and yes, I do understand that democracy is not the perfect system. The US has spent over two hundred years trying to get it right. And returning to Abu Ghraib, those young people did not live up to the standards of our country.'

Arms shot up. The waters had been tested and everyone wished to have their say. Avoiding the necessity for selection, another blurted out:

'So, is the US preparing regime change in Syria?'

The room filled with smirks. Sensing the mockery Juliet added her humour. 'Believe it or not, the US is not in the habit of regime change.' She then continued with the overriding theme that 'the voices of the people of the Middle East should be given the opportunity to determine their own future and the path of their nations.'

She paused and surveyed an unsatisfied crowd. 'Regime change doesn't happen overnight.'

At the back of the room, a solitary figure with a glinting, nasty looking smile relished the reaction he knew he would elicit. He calmly laid down a statement, watching for the desired reaction. Other students knowingly held their breath.

'I support the killing of the American marines in 1983. They were armed soldiers on Lebanese soil. I support the killing, and I am the voice of the Lebanese people.'

The students looked to each other with a mixture of horror and excitement. The antagonistic student was referring to the Iranian-backed bombing of the American Embassy. Although linked to the wider Hezbollah framework, the attack was carried out by the group Islamic Jihad. Added to which Mustapha Mohammed Najjar, Iran's then Defence Minister personally delivered the explosives to the militants. Attention shifted back to the stage, the crowd eagerly awaiting Juliet's response with which she undermined her interlocutor acquiring the sympathies of the majority, by calmly replying:

'I hope you search your soul and don't carry that philosophy with you when you build a platform for your new nation.'

She quickly twitched her head to the crowd asking for further questions before her attacker could think of a comeback. By this point, the focus of the discussion was now firmly hitched to Hezbollah as a more deferential *hijabi* girl rose from her chair:

'Hezbollah are the resistance against Israeli occupation. You started the talk asking us to look away from the past, but now you are criticizing Hezbollah for *their* past actions.'

She did not want to be associated with the previous man and looked sympathetically towards Juliet concluding:

'I do not support Hezbollah.'

Juliet comically pretended to pull her hair out in exasperation:

'What are Hezbollah doing to serve Lebanon?'

Hands shot up as voices chirped in unison: 'Schools, hospitals.' Their united front demonstrated the success of Hezbollah's social service provisions. During the civil war, the party had won much support both within the loyal Shia community and across the wider Lebanese society, by providing vital services that the inconspicuous government could not. At the same time, many saw Hezbollah as the only means of defence against the largely hated Israeli military presence that continued to loiter on Lebanon's southern border.

The Lebanese had learned to be realists, and knew that the Iranian-funded Hezbollah services came with strings attached. Iran and a smaller Syrian contribution kept medical centres and schools ticking over. Both nations had a vested interest in keeping the fight with Israel alive. Syria may have feared for her own borders but I continued to think that for Iran, antagonizing the Israelis was a classic means of distracting the Iranian people from more serious domestic problems. Essentially, both nations craved a hate figure, and the Hezbollah's guerrilla tactics kept up the much needed Israeli aggression.

Juliet knew this all too well and played on the Lebanese hatred of foreign intervention:

'Yep, but do they serve the Lebanese?'

She paused to allow them to mull over her question before finishing with:

'They serve the Iranians and their agenda. Hezbollah don't have a real desire to help *you*, the Lebanese people.'

Others disagreed. The men continued to dominate as another shouted:

'How can you answer for the fact that Israel continually violates the Lebanese border?'

The question stemmed from the generally held opinion that America was responsible for the actions of their lapdog, Israel, an argument Juliet often faced. She dutifully replied:

'We do actually tell the Israeli Government not to violate Lebanese air space and territories.'

Her voice best disguised her frustration that the responsibility for Israeli misdemeanours was frequently laid at America's feet.

It was not simply the threat to Lebanon's southern border that angered these Lebanese students. Though few would ever admit it publically, there was a deep resentment among the Lebanese who perceived the arrival of 700,000 Palestinian refugees in 1948 and the subsequent PLO leadership as an invasion which triggered their lengthy civil war.

A tall, pretty girl hoped the upcoming UN Resolution 1559 would address this concern:

'Will this resolution open the door to the Palestinian people? We have had a 30-year civil war trying to get the Palestinians out of our country, a country in which they do not belong.'

Juliet undermined the all-powerful Israeli image whilst directing the class's attention to the nature of Resolution 1559:

'Firstly, the Israelis don't have a seat on the Security Council. Secondly, Resolution 1559 had nothing to do with Israel. It's between Syria and Lebanon. It's about getting Syrian troops out of Lebanon. Palestinian refugees are not included.'

The subject of the Palestinians gave Juliet the perfect opportunity to state what many in the Middle East seemed to forget, that the illusion of 'Arab brotherhood' between more sedentary Arab nations and the itinerant Palestinians was a myth.

'The Palestinians have become a tool. They are used as a means of diversion by your own politicians and other Arab governments. The Palestinian issue is brought up again and again in the Middle East to distract you from the real problems in society. Everyone does it, but who do you think benefits the least from it?'

Despite the obvious conclusion, unthinking faces stared back at the stage. Juliet looked increasingly exasperated: 'The Palestinians'.

Forty minutes had passed in which time Juliet had largely held her own. Once the circular Palestinian discussion had been given a thorough airing, a tubby, friendly looking man unravelled her central maxim: Freedom in Democracy.

'You talk of democracy and 'empowering' the people of the Middle East, yet why does your government continue to support Hosni Mubarak and his dictatorship regime?'

This was a question of which my Egyptian friend, Sharifah, would have certainly approved. It was at this stage when diplomacy and the separation of the individual from the state occurred. Juliet was all too aware of her predicament, wryly smiling she replied:

'In essence, you're getting down to the crux of what's difficult. As Americans we have ideals, although sometimes we don't manage to live up to them. Mubarak has been a strong ally of the US, but I can understand your argument that the US has turned a blind eye to Egypt.'

Although it was a question only George Bush Jnr's administration could adequately answer, I felt the US had some room for defence. I raised my hand to embrace the 'special relationship', although I failed to be picked out in a Mexican wave of enthusiastic hands.

I felt it was naive not to realize that any superpower was

stuck in a quagmire of criticism by never reaching a balance between isolationism and meddling in the affairs of others. My hand and thoughts fell to the floor as the Lebanese students debated the future of their country at the hands of their countrymen.

On 12th July 2006 Hezbollah fired rockets at Israeli border towns in a diversionary tactic before ambushing two armoured Israeli Humvees patrolling the Israeli-Lebanon border. This was the start of the Israeli-Hezbollah *July War* that saw the deaths of over 1,200 people, including between 6-9 individuals from the Iranian Revolutionary Guard and the displacement of thousands within both Lebanon and Israel.

Trolls in the mist.
Great Arab conspiracy theories

Aleppo, Syria
April 14

The steam and friction rolled arms with dead skin reminiscent of long, soaking baths. Sweat breached my eyebrows stinging my eyes. I sat alone in Aleppo's famous bath house, the Hammam Yalbougha An-Nasry, hiding in a steamy room that hissed out hot water vapour like a budget horror film's torture finale.

My visibility was reduced to a metre. I felt nervous recollecting the Turkish bath scene in 'Day of the Jackal'. The dense steam cloud muffled the clapping noises of wooden sandals against the tiled floor.

The hammam's humid dungeon was run by a draconian troll of a man. He was a short, stocky, steroid-driven beast with a sadistic smile. He lurked in the mist and caught his 'customers' for a routine 'massage' of pain. Like 'The Phantom of the Opera', he suddenly appeared from his secret lair and grabbed my bowl with a grunt calling me to follow.

At the foot of the hammam's stone stairs, the nightmare began. My body braced in premature fear as the 'troll' pulled onto his trotter a thick glove pasted with a substance resembling pumice. With an iron grip he seemed to extract my arms from their sockets before pinching my muscles in his vice-like grip, happily sanding away at my skin. I could almost hear the tight muscle fibres rip above my pathetic whimpers.

My raw skin exuded a beetroot colour as exposed pores itched like a parasitically victimised dog. No, it was still not enough. The troll wished to increase the flea sensation further by lathering a bar of soap and rubbing once more. I realised in horror that the pain would not end until my entire body had been thoroughly bruised.

Perhaps I had misunderstood the concept of a massage. I recalled comfortable sterile shoulder massages in the school's sanatorium addressing bone-breaking knocks from the toff-hating Bristol Grammar under-14s rugby matches.

The troll gripped my legs. His hands acted as piercing needles running up and down my tender calves. Feeling exposed, I was commanded to lie on my front as he jabbed between each vertebrae. He seemed a chiropractor's dream, generating wealth as he leant his bodyweight against my weak shoulder blades.

I continued to emit effeminate puppy-like yelps. The troll ignored my pleas, repeating the whole ritual a second time, with a further opportunity of proving his male prowess.

As my face was forcibly pressed down onto the hammam tiles, I imagined the thousands of verucca-infested feet that had trodden before me. I imagined trolls past. He was without doubt a veteran of Afghanistan's Arab *mujahideen* brigades.

After an honourable discharge, he had relocated to conduct a special torture posting in Aleppo in a pre-emptive move to paralyse any Westerners who dared enter his abode.

After the torture I sat feeling relieved, sucking an apple shesha water pipe in the hammam's foyer nursing my wounds. My persecuted predecessor from the dungeon of pain stopped at my table to tie his shoe laces. He looked up and introduced himself as Hamik, a Jordanian businessman.

Our conversation developed to expose some amusing Arab points of view. Hamik enjoyed announcing his views in a conspiratorial manner. We started with 9/11. 'I tell you, it was a CIA plot. I have a good friend who flies aeroplanes and he tells me that two planes could never cause so much damage. When you look at the television pictures, look at the first plane … it flies into the building and then there is a moment before the explosion.' Hamik attributed this to 'very clever camera work.'

As with many political exchanges in the Middle East, the omnipotent Jews- came under fire. 'Another thing, do you know about the Jews in 9/11?' I tried to look surprised and willing to believe: 'No, tell me.'

'No Jew turned up to work that day. They all knew it was going to happen. I promise you it is true. It was in all the newspapers.' Later on I did some internet research and found that Hamik was partially correct. The latter was true. The Saudi newspaper *Al-Watan* imagined the story which soon spread to Hezbollah's *Al-Manar* news channel and was cordially accepted by many as gospel.

We had a brief lull in our conversation as I thought of other home truths to be extracted. Lacking quick thinking, I reverted to 9/11 again. 'But, Hamik, why would the CIA do that?' Without a second thought he burst back at me: 'What do you think? They did it as an excuse to invade Iraq. They are greedy, the Americans. They want Iraq's oil and needed an excuse to attack. They then tried to make people believe it was right with talk of these weapons. But tell me, where are they now?'

Leaving the hammam, we came out to the cafes surrounding Aleppo's third millennium BC citadel. The castle was beautifully illuminated at night with powerful lights shining up onto the outer walls. We sat with Turkish coffees as Hamik told me more of his trade as an antiquities dealer with a shop and a well-placed mistress on London's Fulham Road. He left the table and opened his Suzuki's glove compartment, returning with two small golden coins. 'See these? One is real and one is fake. Here in Aleppo, they are very good at forging genuine Syrian antiquities. But I want you to guess which one is real.' I turned them over again and again, inspecting their colour and surface for wear and tear. Thinking it to be a trick question I held the newer looking of the two up to the light, proudly announcing: 'This one is genuine.' Hamik took it from me. 'Wrong, it is this one,' pointing to the other in my hand. 'Look at the edges. Look at the little cuts.' Little teeth marks bit around the coin's circumference. 'This is done by a thief. He would have shaved little bits off each coin until he had enough to forge a new coin.'

Pointing up to the castle, Hamik gestured to the source of his gold coins. 'I have bought hundreds of these coins. They were all found in the castle. I bought them with many other things for 20 million dollars. I'll sell most at auctions in London and in my shop.'

We moved back to Middle Eastern politics and focussed our energies on the Israelis once more. Hamik had no doubt as to who was responsible for Rafiq Al Hariri's death. Unlike the Lebanese people I was soon to meet, Hamik pointed the finger of blame south of the border. 'Of course it was Sharon and the Israelis. They killed him and you know why?' I gave him the answer he was wishing for: 'Because they knew the Syrians would be blamed. Then America and the Lebanese would call for Syria to withdraw.' Hamik beamed from ear to ear, he looked pleased to have passed his knowledge onto his new protégé. He leant across the table to shake my hand in congratulations. 'Charlie, you are a clever man. Exactly. The Israelis are angry with Syria, because they help Hezbollah to fight in south Lebanon. Every man has his ways of vengeance and this is theirs.'

Module 2:
Minorities in the region

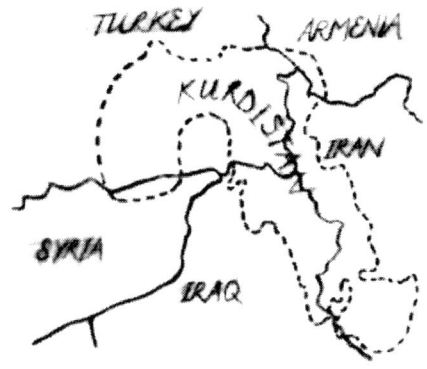

Mehvec Kenan and the Kurdish 'problem'

Diyarbakir, Turkey
September 6

In front of the city's threatening black basalt walls, a wedding party zoomed past. The bride and groom's car streaked with white and red flapping ribbons. A motorcade followed as dozens of revellers leant out of their car windows, flashing their lights with a poorly co-ordinated racket of beeping horns.

Despite the sinister reputation, Diyarbakir had changed course and was now considered a 'peaceful' city. Even so, the racket awoke the uneasy authorities, as a 4×4 loaded with a section of rifle-clutching troops swept away into the evening darkness after the fading wedding party. I passed an old man outside the city's dark walls. He slept snoring in the dry flower beds, homeless and oblivious of the festivities.

'The next thing you'll see will be a blood feud in this town,' came a dismissive voice from the square. A Kurdish journalist from Istanbul, Mehvec Kenan stood there referring to the old feudal practice, whereby honour and violence collided into a murderous vortex that saw whole families obliterated. A cigarette glowed from Mehvec's fingers, he looked tired staggering up the square's stone steps.

'What's that supposed to mean?' I replied, as we greeted each other warmly.

'Well, you know the Kurds are still a bloody and savage lot?' He joked. 'But seriously, I get sick of this barbarism. Even in Istanbul I have seen cars chasing after each other in attempts to revenge a death.'

The city seemed uncomfortably still that night. Mehvec's cigarette smoke hung in the air as he exhaled. The pattering of a plastic football echoed around the square from a group of boys involved in a hugely competitive game. I had not been travelling for long, but I already knew the people to avoid: police, pickpockets and any boys older than 5, who often had much to do with both professions.

I asked Mehvec about an incident I had experienced earlier that day at the bus stop. I sat waiting on the bench when a swift urchin sidled up, grabbed and tried to sprint off with my map. His friends huddled together, rejoicing at the spectacle of antagonising a tourist.

'You see here, Charlie, the children have no childhood. Believe me, if you were raised in Diyarbakir, you would grow up fast. These children have to work from very early on in life. And you must have seen the illegal settlements where most of them live?'

I had. That afternoon I had circumnavigated the city walls, looking out onto a skyline of red bricks and concrete jerry-built houses, TV aerials branching from flimsy, rusty roofs.

'There is no work here. There's nothing to do. Its hardly surprising that many young people start taking drugs.

Diyarbakir has some of the purest and cheapest heroin available. It all comes from the across the border in Iran. The children here have the first pick. All of the heroin that comes into Europe comes along this route from eastern Turkey.'

Irrespective of drugs, Diyarbakir had become a byword for terror in Turkey. Despite Turkey's near nationwide enforcement of extraordinary rule since 1940, Diyarbakir along with her seven neighbouring provinces fell victim to the guerrilla activities of the Kurdish Workers Party, better known as the PKK. The Kurdish nationalist group had ruffled the insecurities of the Turkish Government and population alike since the late 1970s, fomenting the bitter ethnic conflict that still persists today. In 1987, the government placed this cluster of rotten provinces in a special administrative area known as OHAL, whereby a regional governor oversaw a state of emergency and enforced many accompanying draconian measures.

'But I thought everything had returned to normal now?' I ventured.

'The government isn't so heavy handed, or at least do not appear to be and the electricity cuts and night curfews are gone, although people's lives haven't necessarily improved. The past still haunts every rock of this city.'

Mehvec paused for a point of reference.

'OK. Today, I had to go out of town and interview Kurds living in practically deserted villages. We were asking them about the effects of the government displacement policies.' He looked up to see my blank, ignorant face.

'The PKK used the mountain villages for safe houses and food caches. Of course, the Turkish army realised what was going on and cleared the entire local population from these areas so that the insurgents had no one to rely on. Still today villages remain uprooted, their inhabitants near refugees in their own land.'

* * *

We walked into the dark, menacing city, as the night's sky disappeared into a labyrinth of alleys where adolescents walked aimlessly, hawking boxes of cigarettes, watches and batteries. A café emitted locust clicks of dominos loudly colliding with their boards, the dimly lit rooms heaved with old men chain smoking in a collective effort to add further smog to the rooms' communal smoke clouds that wafted up to the ceilings. A few paces on the clicking stopped, as the streets' irregular turns and twists muffled the nocturnal sounds.

Mehvec lead me to a small patisserie where inside a portly shopkeeper awkwardly unbuttoned his apron and welcomed us in, before cleaning down the glass surfaces for another day, handing us a plate of sticky sweets and pastries.

Taking a *baklava*, Mehvec started to talk about his life. It was a story of immense drive, an improbable tale of a Kurdish nomad who strove to become a reporter for the prestigious Turkish News Agency.

'I didn't want to be nomadic for the rest of my life. It was boring. I didn't see the point,' he said.

I questioned the family pressures that must have exerted themselves upon a determined academic.

Mehvec softly laughed: 'You're right. It was hard, but I was lucky. There was only one thing to do. I had to become an educated man. And again I was lucky, my family were very accepting that I didn't want to be a nomad and they allowed me to study. Eventually I went to university in Ankara, and then the real challenge began. I lived in a tiny flat which I shared with six other students. There were no walls to divide the rooms, only huge glass sheets. So we had to stick newspapers across the glass for privacy. And here I am now, living and working in Istanbul.'

I craved to hear of some rustic existence, asking 'and are your family still nomadic?'

Mehvec sadly concluded his story with more modern eventualities. 'No, my mother and father gave up that way of life some time ago. My uncle and aunt are still nomads. I sometimes go back to visit them for a few days. But you know, I don't like to be there too long. I see the same people I knew as a child sitting in the same cafés, smoking the same cigarettes, playing the same game of dominoes. We always greet each other warmly, but now I have nothing in common with them.'

It was sad to hear Mehvec talk about these paralysed family reunions. The rather patronising orientalist in me wished it were not the case; rather that others who followed what I perceived to be a romantic and rural existence, continued to trample the land, moving as livestock and the seasons decreed.

The shopkeeper soon ceased to possess his earlier rotund charm and started to strain at his watch and comically attempt subtle shakes of his head, beckoning us to the door. The debonair nomad charmed him to stay open for a little longer, coercing him to bring two more Turkish coffees, scalding hot, thick and sweet … 'Sloane Ranger' qualities in the caffeine form.

The coffees came at a price as Mehvec turned the focus of the inquisition on me.

'Go ahead! I want to see what you think about the 'Kurds' after all your time in Turkey.' He spat the words out in a feigned disgust and lit another cigarette.

I began my elementary assessment, that back in Britain the Kurdish question was usually presented more as a Guardianesque 'Kurdish problem', as a sympathy-evoking nationalist cause that pre-occupied our Sunday newspaper supplements. A colonialist contriteness appealed to a people, who, like so many in the Middle East had fallen victim to the beguiling Sykes-Picot Treaty of 1916.

I went on, explaining to Mehvec my swift re-education on the subject having been at the harsh end of an Ephesus tour guide's diatribe in Seljuk, a loud and dominant man who objected to my appellation of the 'Kurdish problem'. On hearing this definition, the guide firmly informed me that Turkey was a multiracial nation that included Anatolian Turks, Greeks, Armenians and Arabs. The Kurds to him were simply another 'Turkish' group, not an alien race that possessed the right to force Turkey's fragmentation due to their parochial nationalist feelings.

Mehvec interrupted, 'That is typical. In Istanbul, as expected, I have a lot of very 'liberal' minded friends, but as soon as anyone utters a reference to the Kurdish 'question', they become practically fascist.'

Whilst hiding his own beliefs, Mehvec allowed room for his friend's momentary outburst. 'Yet after years of fighting the PKK, you must understand their anger. You know how much it costs for the government to fight the PKK? Some people have put the estimates over the last 10 years to $100 billion US, and that's only the financial cost. Most Turks haven't forgotten the human loss, over 30,000 have been killed.'

Due to compulsory military service in Turkey, I had met many men in their late 30s and early 40s who had all been actively involved in quashing the PKK's activities. When I first arrived in Turkey, a distant colleague of my mother's, who bargained in au pairs for the home counties' middle classes, kindly had me to stay. The unfortunately named 'Ufuk' a qualified medical doctor, often recounted his days in the field hospital when all hell was breaking loose. At the time, in the mid-1990s, some sections of Turkish society were awash with a greatly accepted rumour that the Kurdish insurgency was directly receiving American military aid. Ufuk swore that he had seen American helicopters dropping off such supplies to the PKK.

On hearing the story, Mehvec was sceptical. 'I have heard people saying these things many a time. Yet, I really don't think there's much truth in the matter. However, there are many other things the United States and your government have done to upset this part of the world.' I felt vicarious guilt as one often does on hearing such remarks.

'When George Bush Snr encouraged Kurdish uprisings in Iraq after he had defeated Saddam in the first Gulf War, the Americans still allowed Iraqi helicopters to fly and continue their bombing campaign on the revolutionary Kurdish areas. This carried on even when the British tried to help.' Mehvec was referring to the 1991 Royal Marine lead 'Operation Safe Haven' which disembarked in Diyarbakir providing regional security in northern Iraq for Kurdish refugees fleeing Saddam's attacks.

'Despite that, over two million Iraqi Kurds fled to Turkey and lived in atrocious refugee camps. We even have one here in Diyarbakir. These people were left to live in terrible conditions, without any hope of employment. Once the world's press got bored and moved on, the Iraqi Kurds could not. They had to stay behind these fences as virtual prisoners in a 'host' country.'

Slightly defensively I said, 'So you are not a fan of the US and Britain then?'

Mehvec shook his head, thinking of how best to explain his views to a politically biased English adolescent, before surprising me with digs at his own nation and her Ataturk-inspired pride. 'With the British, I have few problems. In my opinion it is the Americans who share surprising parallels with the Turkish people. Both nations can be patriotic to a ridiculous extent, and eventually both people become so proud, they become openly aggressive in their arrogance. It is not hard for a country to think they're the best and everyone else is inferior.'

His crescendo dropped into a self-deprecating finale. 'But one thing I am sure of, is that I would be scared to go to the countries you are going to.' I felt growing unease at these words. Were they praise at my foolhardy mission or a teacher's admonishment to his pupil on a subject of which he knows little?

Mehvec receded into the darkness as we left for our respective hotels. His faceless words hung in the anonymity of night. 'Don't forget what they say, Charlie: God Bless America! Pity everyone else.'

* * *

The next night I sat mulling over Mehvec's words, sitting in a state of enormous self-pity as I froze on a bus with leaking windows and sodden seats. We crept slowly east towards Van, interrupted by machine gun-mounted police check points that ordered all previously dormant passengers out. All ID was meticulously studied whilst our bus was ransacked for drugs.

I felt an ambivalent pity for the Kurds, a people who had been overlooked when the Whitehall maps and rulers had first met, although simultaneously their struggle to me seemed futile. That was not to say they were not entitled to a 'homeland' of some sort. Rather though, that the military and cultural opposition to their plight from Turkey, Syria and Iran was unlikely to dissolve. While Kurdish nationalism may be a useful tool for cementing a section of Iraq's heterogeneous population, it is unlikely to be used effectively in efforts to unite a homogenous and successful post-Saddam Iraq.

The Palestinian refugees of Shatila

West Beirut, Lebanon
April 27

'I have not been here for 15 years!' The taxi driver flung his hands into the air with despair. We stopped every few minutes to get our bearings from wandering pedestrians. A 'camp' sounds peripheral, yet 'Shatila' was an ethnically exclusive area close to the centre of Beirut. For four generations, Palestinians had lived in the area, ever since they had fled Galilee, today's northern Israel, during the 1948 Arab–Israeli war. Sprawling Beirut had grown around Shatila, engulfing the area and other Palestinian camps, camps that many thought to be temporary. The Palestinian optimism that one day they would return to their villages remained for decades. Today, they are still called 'camps', but they are now permanent.

The old Mercedes churned slowly through a poor suburb. 'Here many, many Hezbollah', my Christian taxi driver chuckled, waving his hands in indication across the dashboard.

For the first time in Beirut I saw beggars at the side of the road. Wheelchair-ridden men blocked the lanes at roundabouts. Old ladies stood, stooped with thin, wrinkled palms and five twig-like fingers outstretched for money. Each beggar held their heads bowed down, eyes transfixed on the road.

The area was the backwater of Beirut. Litter and people drifted aimlessly in the street. Pictures of martyrs to the cause hung on A4 boards attached to street lamps. The Iranian cleric, Ayatollah Khomeini, and the Hezbollah Lebanese leader, Hassan Nasrallah, smiled at each other across the streets above car workshop canopies and falafel stands. White-turbaned Imams demonstrated their equanimity in Allah controlling Beirut's traffic as they crossed the roads without turning to look.

We looped along the same stretches of road, until the camp appeared from the centre of our oscillations. Initially, I could not distinguish Shatila from the previous poverty of pot-holed roads and encroaching rubbish dumps. I did not know quite what to expect. The night before I had conjured up images of Kalashnikov-wielding PLO warriors standing stoically behind razor wire fences encircling a bustling tent city.

My premonitions were a little Hollywoodesque. The camp had seen a turnover of four generations since 1948. Tents had long been abandoned. Bricks and mortar cemented the more realistic prospects for Palestine's refugees. The camp was a mess of high-rise, unplanned housing blocks with occasional modern-looking apartments.

My disorientated Christian driver departed as quickly as he could. Two Palestinian taxi drivers seemed unbothered at my arrival, leaning up against their cars smoking and chatting. I asked for the 'Health Centre' shrugging my shoulders. They looked at me and then at each other. 'Engleesee' came the reply as they pointed to a tall young man in his twenties who stood outside a vegetable stall. He understood and pointed down an alley, wiggling his hand to indicate the intended route. I should take a right, go straight and a right again. I followed his instructions down the alleyway. I watched underfoot avoiding exposed pipes and puddles that stagnated in concrete depressions along the lane's unevenly spread cement path. My shoulders were scraping along thinly plastered breeze-block walls. Cats sat upon rubbish heaps meowing at my passing. A group of children skipped past, barging their way through the thin pass, hopping at all the right places with full knowledge of the irregularities of the concrete, which like their lives seemed uncertain and treacherous.

I arrived at the Red Crescent Health Centre. Thankfully, they had my contact's namesake a 'Mr Maarouf,' although they soon worked out that I needed the other Mr Maarouf, a different Mr Maarouf who worked at a different healthcare centre, that of the United Nations. I felt guilty following an old lady who led me away to the UN centre. She stooped, accommodating her crooked back with every step appearing painful.

A small white 'UN Refugee Agency' sign welcomed me inside, where three men huddled around a small *sheesha* chatting and smoking in a bare office. The deputy of the health centre sat trapped up against the wall by his empty office desk. He courteously invited me in to wait for the boss, the genuine Mr Maarouf.

'Hello, Mr Leigh. Yes, I am Mr Maarouf. I am responsible for health, sanitation and education here in Shatila.' He arrived, well dressed with a smartly ironed shirt and tie, but his face failed to hide his entrenched boredom. I imagined myself to be one of many visitors that month. It was obvious that despite all the articles written, few things seemed to change. Mr Maarouf had the unenviable job of escorting all romantically inclined journalists on camp tours, a chore his three juniors seemed eager to avoid as they remained smoking in the office.

After two minutes I was already asking him about the keys that some occupants of Shatila and Sabra, a neighbouring Palestinian camp, had kept since they left their homes in 1948. This was a famous anecdote of the fleeing Palestinians who had locked the doors to their homes before moving north in the hope of returning shortly.

'There are very few keys now. Most people left Palestine in a hurry and left them in the locks.' The laconic Mr Maarouf quickly quelled my eager queries and continued in the same vain showing little enthusiasm for my questions.

We walked through the streets where electricity lines and thick, black plastic water pipes crisscrossed over our heads. He noticed my wandering eyes and spoke in an unemotional, matter of fact way. 'We are not allowed drinking water here. Our main tank was destroyed in the war and the government hasn't bothered to build a new one. All water runs from house to house along these black pipes. It is only the UN who provide services here.'

Challenging him I pointed to a water tank that had been sprayed with a stencil of the Iranian flag. Mr Maarouf quickly readdressed the matter. 'And Hezbollah give us a few things.'

'Surely, the people here know that their old homes in Palestine are largely owned by Israelis now?' He looked angry when I asked the obvious question that begged for a quotable response. He spoke with a rehearsed monotony, as though quoting some fictional event. 'Yes, we know this. If and when we go back we are all going to reconstruct our homes or build new homes.'

Traders pushed tables of lemons on trolleys made from wooden planks fixed with bicycle wheels. Their eyes flickered to the ground as they navigated over the bumps and holes that might upset their precious yellow cargo. On the street corners, young men sat chatting idly. Seeing them, Mr Maarouf spoke:

'These people have nothing to do here, especially the young men. You asked me which jobs aren't permitted for Palestinians in Lebanon. Well, nearly all jobs, nearly all the best ones. It is inconceivable to think that we could ever become lawyers, doctors or engineers.'

A strong odour of kerosene and diesel lingered in the street air. We passed under the sign 'Palestinian Engineers Organisation'. I pointed to it, attempting to challenge Mr Maarouf with an example of professional Palestinians in Shatila. Before I had time to speak he predicted opposition. 'Don't you see? They can only work in the camp.'

Deeper into the camp, I again noticed the more prosperous, modern-looking apartment blocks. Their window frames had been crudely constructed with cement instead of more expensive metal or plastic materials. We came to a street wall that had been smashed with wide bullet holes. 'Are all these bullet holes from the massacre in 1982?', I asked.

The September 16, 1982 was a date all but the young in Shatila remembered only too well. The Israeli Defence Force violated ceasefire and evacuation plans by suddenly entering West Beirut. Shatila and Sabra were encircled as the Israelis watched from the sidelines while their Lebanese Christian allies, the *Phalangists*, entered both camps and slaughtered any Palestinians in sight, irrespective of age or gender.

Frowning at the thought, Mr Maarouf considered his professional responsibilities before setting down his legal restrictions. 'Mr Leigh, I work for the United Nations. Therefore, I cannot comment on any political issues. I serve the UN and their policies. I am sorry, but I can't tell you when these bullet holes were made. But I can assure you that in Lebanon there have been many opportunities.'

I later learnt that many of Shatila's bullet scars had actually come about during the later 1985–86 camp wars. These events flew in the face of the increasingly circumspect notion of 'Arab Brotherhood'. Simply put, the Syrian president, Hafez Al-Assad, had feared for his minority *Alawite* regime against the increasing power of the Sunni PLO and their leader, Yasser Arafat. Despite largely expelling the PLO from Syria in 1982, Assad played on the Lebanese *Shia* community's resentment towards the Palestinians by sponsoring the powerful *Shia Amal* militia to dislodge Arafat sympathizers in the Beirut camps. The siege started with the cutting off of all supplies entering the camps before *Amal* artillery continually shelled the area in joint operations with a *Shia* brigade from the Lebanese army.

A little boy looked untroubled by the bullet-smeared streets all around him. Thumping a plastic drum, he took joy in scaring a cat out from under a turquoise 1970s Mercedes. Another little boy who looked about four, clambered onto his grandfather's lap. He reached out his hands to me, beckoning me to photograph him. Shatila's children turned out to be professional posers. They all waited politely without fidgeting. On hearing the camera shutter click, they would smile in confirmation. An elder brother appeared from a sliding metal door, affectionately watching his younger sibling hogging the limelight. He lacked Mr Maarouf's forced political neutrality and happily talked away. 'The Lebanese Government have little influence here, although they used to! They once had police in the camp, I think?' He turned to Mr Maarouf for affirmation.

'Yes, one station and three policemen,' Mr Maarouf officially acknowledged. The teenager spoke again, 'But you know the Syrians left Lebanon yesterday?' I nodded. 'Well now the Lebanese Government may wish to get involved in Shatila's lawlessness.'

I wondered what he meant by 'Shatila's lawlessness'? Both men sensed my curiosity. The young man continued. 'Lawlessness! … That is what the Lebanese say, when they have no control over us, the Palestinians. Syria controlled the Lebanese government and the army. So, with them gone, we might see change.'

Mr Maarouf came back to the issue later on, by the northern edges of the camp. He wished to make sure I had not misunderstood the boy's comments. 'There is no lawlessness here. We have little crime as everyone knows each other. When and if there is trouble, we resolve it peacefully.'

Leaving the camp we both looked over to the other side of the road, to an area of wooden huts and tarpaulin rooves. Children sat above the road on the flattened remains of house foundations. Like crushed cans, the houses had been utterly flattened. Ceilings met floors as both were sandwiched together. Rebar metal foundation wires protruded like squashed spiders' legs from the concrete pancakes. Mr Maarouf explained, 'These people are both Lebanese and Syrians who have been displaced since the war. You can see they live in conditions worse than those in Shatila. The whole area was once a forest. But these people cleared the woods and they live here now.' Dirt clouds twisted in little vortexes which ran down soil paths dividing the ramshackle shelters. 'They are waiting for compensation from the government.'

I looked at Mr Maarouf walking slowly back into the concrete camp. I asked him one final question.

'Will the Palestinians ever receive any compensation for their troubles during the Lebanese civil war?' He turned, said nothing, and shook his head. I thanked him and promised to send some photos once I had returned to England.

* * *

Around the camp, the dull grey concrete and breeze blocks acted as a canvas for political messages. Everyone had the same concern: to return to Palestine. Jagged knives in the shape of Palestine cut through bulging pink hearts that oozed blood trickling from the blade. The standard message was a Palestine flag flying high above Jerusalem's Dome of the Rock. A hand reached up behind the dome with a fist clenching a Kalashnikov.

Less political paintings warned of health issues. Like a boa constrictor wrapping around its prey, a cigarette suffocated a more realistic looking heart. I was surprised to see a simple painting of a young man with a sleeve pulled back and a handkerchief tied around his arm holding a syringe in one hand. Opiates must have offered a distraction from the monotony of unemployment.

A group of young shopkeepers shouted loudly as, camera bared, I snapped away at a bulldozer destroying the shell of a dilapidated, war-weary house. The house looked as though it had been a firing position during conflict as thousands of bullet marks peppered the walls.

Other buildings lacked corners which had been eroded by decades of artillery shelling. In one case, their occupants had drawn a canvas screen across to cover a missing wall, rather like a shower curtain.

The edges of Shatila were not all remnants of a conflict. A butcher stood chopping up a huge leg of meat in a beautiful alley, canopied with vines that twisted their leafy foliage on wires crossing the street. A grinning old man stood on a wooden ladder, smashing a plaster wall with a small pointy hammer. He seemed to enjoy being photographed, smiling to show his missing teeth.

A younger, middle-aged man bent over the boot of an old Mercedes taxi, reattaching the vehicle's spare tyre. Scattered tools jingled on the back seat.

'You are English, yes?' He asked. I nodded.

'Good, I am Danish. You would like a taxi? Yes?' He smiled at my acceptance, collecting his tools. Firing up the old workhorse of a Mercedes, we pulled off past the outskirts of the camp as he began to introduce himself. He knew what interested visiting foreigners clutching cameras and note pads.

'My name is Nasim. I was here in 1982 when the *Phalangists* attacked Shatila.'

'And did they try to kill you?' I asked. He looked unfazed.

'No. They would have, but I had a gun. Many people still have guns here. They came entering from the … err … what do you call it? The place where dead people are buried?'

'A graveyard.' I replied.

'Yes, that's it, they entered from the graveyard and I was helping in the fight against them. We held them back for three days. Eventually we were tired and all the armed men left at 5.00 pm on the 19th September.' I quickly realized that the first personal pronoun, 'we' referred to the PLO.

'After that the *Phalangists* entered, they came in and started to kill everyone. As I said I got out early on, but the Israelis arrested me on the Saturday and I was put in prison.'

Nasim stopped, although it did not seem the end of his story. I asked him what happened next.

'I was eventually freed ... because ... do you know that in the Bekaa, we were fighting the Israelis, and we too had some prisoners? So we all swapped. We gave the Israelis back six soldiers, and they gave us twelve hundred Palestinians. I was one of the twelve hundred.' I looked at him with a sceptical face. He laughed.

'I know, it's a lot! Twelve hundred for six!'

By now we had reached the cornice, well away from Hezbollah's **Shia** strongholds. As we passed Beirut's strange coastal rock formation, the famous **Pigeon Rocks**, Nasim started again.

'Ariel Sharon. He got into a lot of trouble. At the time of the massacre he was Israel's Defence Minister; he was responsible. Everyone defending Shatila at the time could see him at the sports centre, using those ... what ... you know?'

He connected his index finger and thumb, holding them to his eye.

'Ah, binoculars.' I said.

'Yes, binoculars, those, we saw him. He let it all happen.' That particular point seemed hard to believe considering Sharon was in Israel when the massacres were unfolding. I kept this view to myself not wishing to knock Nasim off his course, asking, 'You say you are Danish?'

'I left Lebanon in 1982, the same year as the problems in Shatila.' He pointed to a picture of two girls.

'They are my daughters, eight and nine and a half.'

From a pink background, two little girls smiled out of a 'Snoopy' picture frame attached to the dashboard.

'So, why did you comeback?'

'I did not want to come back, but the Danish Government said I had to return to Lebanon, as it was the first country where I became a refugee. They said I was a danger to their national security.'

I tried to find out why. Apart from fighting for the PLO, what had Nasim done? The Danish Government must have had good cause for their caution. Nasim gave no reason. He avoided the issue, continuing:

'I was sent back to Lebanon. The police here met me at the airport and I was put in jail for two months. I had to pay some people in the government and they eventually let me go, but still I cannot go back to Denmark.'

'But surely there will be a court case?' I asked.

'Yes, we started, but, because Hariri died and the Syrians have just left, there is no proper government in Lebanon at the moment. The courts have shut down until the elections, and all cases have been suspended so I don't know what's going to happen.'

Twenty minutes had passed, so I told Nasim I was staying at the US Embassy. This was a particular piece of information I did not want to share back at Shatila. Nasim looked at me in despair. The traffic came to a standstill. He stroked his head in worry and turned to me.

'In Lebanon, Palestinian people like me are treated like animals. The Lebanese tell us to 'go home' all the time, but what can we do? We cannot make any money and Lebanon is far too expensive. I cannot drive this taxi legally. I have to rent it off a Lebanese man.'

'In that case, just drop me here and I'll get another taxi. There will be lots of military checkpoints and police at the Embassy.' Nasim seemed to stop worrying and was seized by a sudden burst of confidence:

'Don't worry, don't worry! It's not a problem. They will not know.'

Approaching the embassy, I realised that the area had been mobilized with hundreds of urban camouflaged soldiers who stood warily around a crowd control water cannon. Outside a hillside café, the usual two sedentary tanks had been fitted with 0.5 heavy machine guns. I could see the embassy poking up from the hilltop. The Lebanese army and police were making their final preparations for the weekly Wednesday Hezbollah anti-American demonstrations. I stuck my head out of the window and 'salaamed' a soldier, who looked no older than me. He acknowledged me and waved the taxi past his checkpoint.

'So, do your family ever come over to see you?'

'No, I do not want them to come here. It is too dangerous, for me, I mean. I am Palestinian, and I could get into trouble with the police if they came here.'

Reaching into my wallet I pulled out 30,000 Lira. It was the correct fare, but I did not have any extra money to give to Nasim.

'And your wife. Is she Palestinian?'

'No, she is Danish. I speak very good Danish. It is the language I use to chat to my daughters.'

I shut the door behind me and handed him the fare.

'But my wife will not be coming here. She separated from me recently.'

* * *

In August 2010, the Lebanese Parliament passed legislation allowing Lebanon's 400,000 Palestinians the same work permits as other 'foreign' workers in the private sector.

Yet Palestinians are still barred from the public sector or professions such as medicine, engineering and law and remain deprived of Lebanese state education or medical services.

Jerusalem and Kahil Kateb

Jerusalem, Israel and the Palestinian territories
May 4

'Give me a chance to rip you off!' A short Palestinian barked to passing tourists from the entrance of his jewellery shop. He had chosen a more original line than the usual, 'Welcome! Welcome! Please come and have a look.' But this man was different from the rest of Jerusalem's Palestinian shopkeepers. This was Kahil Kateb. He stood at about 5 foot 7 inches, a little stocky with a bald shaved head. He spent all day, everyday, looking out of his small cave-shaped shop hoping to sell at least one item. Across the street his father owned a small café, where he too sat outside all day, looking onto the streets, wishing and waiting.

'Ah right you're from London then? I was there in my early twenties. I used to make jewellery and sell it wholesale to the stalls on Portobello Road and Camden Town market. Know what I mean, mate?' Kahil smiled at his convincing cockney accent.

'Anyway, come and 'ave a look. See what I've got to flog …
innit … like'. Fabrics, woven rugs, kilims and pictures covered
the old Jerusalem stone outside his shop. Little wooden
cabinets dangled beautiful Palestinian silver and Eilat
malachite stone bracelets and necklaces. Genuine women's
Bedouin headdresses flopped down from hanging nails in the
walls. Bright colours had been stitched around two small eye
slits that fell to medieval-like armour with a clump of silver
coins running down to cover the remainder of the face. Kahil
gently handed me individual bracelets, all of which he had
made himself. Without my asking, he told me the realities of
his job.

'There is no business anymore. The tourists have stopped
coming and the constant Intifada doesn't help us. Every time
some idiot blows himself up on a bus we are all affected.
Palestinians like me, in Jerusalem, have little hatred for the
Israelis. We're treated well. That's how I got to London.'

'You mean with an Israeli passport?'

Kahil looked at me with disbelief. 'Of course. I could never
travel to London on a Palestinian identity card. We're all lucky.
The passport's great. I can go anywhere I want.'

'But only Jordan and Egypt in the Arab world.' Kahil
laughed. He laughed often. He was an optimist, but one who
knew the difficulties his family would be facing in the future.

'But you know, that the other Palestinians of the West Bank
and Gaza hate us here? They think we've betrayed them
because we live in peace with the Jews.'

Descending a metal staircase from the street above came
one of the many *Haredi* Jews of Jerusalem. Despite having
been there for the best part of a week I was still fascinated by
the way they dressed. The men wore totally black outfits of
shoes, trousers and smart jackets. Their short-cut hair ended

with a small circle cap planted atop. Either side of their face great swirling locks which fell in front of each ear. Kahil smiled as he passed the shop, clasping the man's hands with a warm Hebrew 'Bo-ker Tov' for good morning. The two stood in the street chatting loudly in Hebrew, another language this intelligent Palestinian had mastered. After a few minutes, the man left to carry on with his business.

I was surprised when hearing the two chat. Previously, in Egypt, I had met many Palestinians in exile who vouched never to have had a Jewish friend. It was not necessarily out of a burning hatred, only as they said it was impossible to make friends as both ethnic groups are so different.

'That's crap,' Kahil's concluded as I told him this account. He poured himself another cup of tea from his father's damp kitchen.

'Why do people always believe this? I have many friends who are Jewish, and yes I speak Hebrew. I have lived in Jerusalem all my life and it's an essential language to learn. He is a good man, the one who I just spoke to.'

Kahil pointed to the staircase which his Hasidic friend had just descended. The twisting metal railings rose up to a plateau above David Street. Kahil urged me on.

'Go and have a look. But don't sneak around. They have guards up there'.

Climbing the steps, I came to the plateau above the houses. Bridges ran off the plain, running up to the top levels of houses that were situated with wonderful views over the old city. From then on I would venture up the stairs and sit on a broken wall waiting until sunset, trying to capture the multi-angled shades that cut across the Jerusalem stone. To the west, I could just make out the larger light blue dome of the Church of the Holy Sepulchre with the smaller, drab, brown dome, as well as the tall white tower of the Lutheran Church of the Redeemer behind a mess of satellite dishes and broken orange tiled roofs. The rubble and mish-mash of the compact city blocked my view of most of the Muslim quarter including the 'Via Dolorosa' where lines of tourists marched up and down stopping with their clergyman to inspect each station along the path where Jesus had carried the cross.

Below the eastern sky, I would look across to the Dome of the Rocks' golden casing where according to the Qur'an, Mohammed ascended to heaven. The smaller beige minaret of her neighbour, the Al-Aqsa mosque, peaked up from behind her larger sister. This too was the biblical site of Mount Moraih where Abraham nearly sacrificed his only son, Isaac. The land was sacred to all of the three Abrahamic faiths, where the two temples of Solomon and then Herod once stood, with only the wailing wall a remnant of Herod's temple. From my skyline lookout, I was unable to see the Jewish worshippers who I knew were rocking to and fro against the wailing wall. In the far distance, I could make out the golden teardrop bobbles, like a copy of Moscow's Red Square, a trait that unmistakably gave away the Russian Orthodox church of Mary Magdalene that perched on the fringes of the Mount of Olives.

'Look over there. You see that man?' Kahil had arrived, disturbing my evening tranquillity. He pointed to a small box with a window that rested on top of a large doorway.

'There is an armed guard in that box. He is guarding the entrance to the building and keeping a watchful eye on these rooftops. It is a very strict orthodox area here, you see.' Now that he had pointed him out, I could make out a man staring back at us through binoculars. I did not see the need for such paranoia.

'Well! Why is he doing that? What's there to guard?' I asked. Kahil shrugged his shoulders looking bored.

'They're just scared, keeping a watch over the area. He has got a gun with him … you see only Israelis can have weapons. We, the Palestinians aren't allowed to own firearms.'

He looked at me with a sarcastic grin. 'Cos … you know … we're all terrorists.'

One evening I walked with Kahil out to Zion Gate, through the Armenian quarter, where Kahil's brother had arranged to pick him up and drive him home.

'Old Jerusalem's different religious quarters have become very blurred recently,' started Kahil in a quiet voice forbidding others from eavesdropping.

'You have to be careful what you say in this city. Actually, you have to be careful in this whole country. But you see, here in the Armenian quarter the numbers of Armenians have dropped hugely. Many of the houses are now owned by Jews. Everything is politics here. The more houses any religious group owns in the old city, the bigger their proportion of ownership. Therefore they'll have more votes and that means more power. As an example, my useless little shop's worth about $200,000 US. It's tiny but it'll mean one more property for any religious group.'

He looked around again before continuing.

'It's not just in Jerusalem where the Israelis are buying up land. The new settlements in the West Bank, like the one you saw on the other side of the valley to Bethlehem, they're all made cheaply for the new immigrants.'

I found myself half listening, looking dreamingly at Zion Gate, thinking of the historic events the edifice must have witnessed. The gate looked like a ceiling beam infested with woodworm given the thousands of little bullet holes that shrouded the masonry. A set of three surveillance cameras stood on a post guarding the way. Kahil seemed to read my thoughts.

'You wonder if peace will ever exist here?' He answered his own question. 'I don't know. I think most people are good. As with everything in life, it's always the extremists who ruin it for the rest of us.'

Module 3:
Religion

Mashad. The city of martyrs

Eastern Iran
September 23

Available tickets for the overnight train from Tehran to Mashad in late September were like gold dust. Budhra rang a string of contacts in the railway industry to procure me a seat. With the end of the summer holidays fast approaching, Mashad was filled with pilgrims flocking to one of the holiest sites of Shia Islam, the resting place of the martyred Imam Reza, the eighth of the reverend 12 imams.

I was excited to be taking an old train with cabin compartments to make the 850-km journey east to Mashad. A small television loudly emitted a dubbed version of David Jason's 'A Touch of Frost.' A cleverly installed mirror reflected the drama for the other two travellers who filled the cabin, as we sat staring across at each other.

After a dinner of chicken and rice, the carriage corridor filled with cheers as two musicians started an impromptu concert. One man strummed away at a fragile Iranian lute instrument, an eight-stringed **Tanbur**. His friend rhythmically patted a goblet shaped **Tonbak** drum. Little girls scrambled off their mothers' laps, dancing with twisting arms, snatching the audience's attention and uniting the carriage in the euphoria of their pilgrimage.

After a sleepless night, we arrived in Mashad. I escaped the clutches of persistent taxi drivers and attempted to navigate on foot the way to the Imam Reza complex. My mistake led to hours of appeals for direction to pedestrians at each roundabout.

One man I asked was more forthcoming than most. Unshaven and balding with red betel nut-stained teeth, his narrower eyes betrayed a more Eastern, Afghan origin. He pointed out the correct direction before turning his hand to me, 'Engleezee' he shouted. I nodded. He grabbed my hand in a strong grip and leant forward, crumpling his lips and kissing me vigorously. I jumped back. He loosened his grip, laughed and hobbled along calling repeatedly with a scratchy, tobacco-damaged voice, 'Engleezee … Engleezee.'

I followed Imam Reza Street, which led logically to the complex's many mosque domes and minarets poking out above the buildings of Mashad. The complex was centred around a golden dome. This marked the mausoleum of Imam Reza, surrounded by seven courtyards encompassing the Azim-e Gohar Shad mosque, a library, a cemetery, a museum and a university of Islamic sciences.

Each courtyard was unique though shared common features with tiled walls of sprawling turquoise, navy blue, yellow, green and white floral patterns. Glass chandeliers hung from thirty metre high alcoves illuminating thick blue bands of calligraphied white Qur'anic inscriptions.

In *Azadi* (Freedom) courtyard, laymen jumped to their feet around a central water fountain and approached turbanned mullahs, kissing their hands, exchanging polite words and quickly departing. Men in black walked solemnly balancing open coffins on their shoulders. They entered the shrine of Imam Reza. I could not follow as Christians were not permitted into the mausoleum. The same dark figures soon reappeared with tearful eyes before placing their coffins to the ground so that others could congregate, touch the deceased and join in their mourning.

Pakistanis, Arabs and even African-looking Tanzanians entered Imam Reza's shrine. Their mixed nationalities were examples of the city's ecclesiastical appeal, attracting between fifteen and twenty million visitors a year.

Feeling excluded, I left and went to seek out **Kuh Sangi Park** at the behest of Budhra. I made my way in the rough direction along Daneshgah Street. A rocky hill top marked the start of the park where a staircase led up to a line of women praying, kneeling in the direction of the orange glow of the fading western dusk.

An encirclement of olive green tents obscured the Iranian army's attempt to reconstruct a trench scene from the Iran–Iraq war. Corrugated iron sheets walled the dugout trench where grey, stuffed figures stood motionlessly clutching wooden replica rifles. The city's theme of martyrdom had been recreated with a liberal application of red paint, emphasising the suffering of the Iranian soldiers in the Al-Busrah/Karramashahr marshlands. Screams and gun fire echoed from an embedded cassette player.

At trestle tables, children played with rocket-propelled grenade launchers and Kalashnikovs under the supervision of their parents and bored-looking soldiers. A teenager sat excitedly turning a large anti-aircraft gun, shouting to his friends who clambered in mock withdrawal over a defunct T62 tank.

Walking back towards Imam Reza's shrine, a chatty man beckoned me into his vacant restaurant. I went down to a large subterranean hall and sat down with the owner, a portly Indian Muslim who comically referred to his homeland as 'the rubbish tip of the world.' On hearing I was English, he burst into applause.

'Ah England, wonderful! I worked as a chef in Gloucester Road in 1986 when my wife needed an operation.' We exchanged Kensington street names and landmarks before Mr Jamali gave me a brief narrative of his life. Having left India to make his fortune abroad, he had enlisted in the Shah, Reza Pahlavi's army, working as an assistant to American military advisers rearming and retraining the Shah's beloved forces. With great reverence, Mr Jamali told me of how one generous expatriate American left the entire contents of his flat to him on his departure. Taking advantage of his good fortune, Mr Jamali sold the furniture and raised enough capital to buy his restaurant.

'Soon I will sell this place. The hotel behind this building wants to buy it and accommodate the ever-increasing numbers of pilgrims.' His eyes lit up as he recounted the profit he was soon to accrue. '$600,000 dollars,' he smiled.

A man in his forties came down the steps from the street above and stopped at our table to kiss Mr Jamali on the hands. 'This is my son,' Mr Jamali proudly announced.

His son, Akram, joined us, and without encouragement started to berate the government. 'My son is stupid. He gets into trouble for saying these things.' His father scolded him. Akram seemed disinterested by these paternal warnings and proudly told me of his subversive record with the Ministry of

Information. He spoke of the regional divisions in the sacred city of Mashad. For Akram, the region of **Panjrah** was a desperate area of poverty and opium dependency. The occupants of another area, **Saltiman** hated the government to such an extent that no policeman would dare enter. This situation in turn allowed a 'free trade zone' as he joked, of smugglers and drug dealers who were able to go about their business unhindered.

'But here you are in the city of martyrs,' Akram sneered. 'If you want to see some martyrs go to Behest-e-Reza cemetery.' He stopped without explanation. 'Why?' I asked. 'It is where the government buried all the political enemies they killed after Khomeini's revolution in 1979.'

* * *

The next morning I hailed a taxi and reading the address from a card of phonetically translated words Akram had written for me the night before, I asked to be taken to Behest-e-Reza. The driver shook his head and raised his hands questioning my intent. I insisted, 'Yes, Behest-e-Reza.' He looked confused. I nodded vigorously.

He repeated the words to himself before accepting the destination. We drove out of the city and headed east towards the Afghan border. We soon entered a walled complex by the road side and passed an office and a stinking public lavatory. The road continued past lines of Cypress trees until we came to a crossroads. The driver stopped and indicated he would wait for my return.

I walked on into a patchwork of walled courtyards which enclosed the dead. At first I thought I had come to the wrong cemetery. The courtyards were filled with rectangular green hoods, standing on four legs over mausoleums to deceased clergy. Iranian flags protruded from these small metal canopies which covered stone boxes filled with flowers in bloom, the stonework decorated with Qur'anic inscriptions. Pictures of revered mullahs had been etched into the stone. Fresh wreaths had been dotted around the tombs as two gardeners swept the ground and watered well-maintained borders of flowers and trees.

I continued into the next courtyard. The tombs had been reserved for the martyrs of the Iran–Iraq war. They were more modest than the former clergy. Pill boxes stood on metal legs above elevated white marble grave covers. Inside the pill boxes, small curtains concealed photographs of the sacrificed young men staring determinedly into the camera. Plastic red roses rested by the photos, their colour faded by the sunlight. Other martyrs' graves had framed paintings and larger pictures which stood defiant in the evening breeze.

Across the road a car arrived. An elderly couple got out and gave me vicious stares. I left and veered down the road in an attempt to avoid further confrontations. The road continued past courtyards of less honoured individuals. The common man, not a mullah or a martyr, had been issued a standard white marble grave etched with familiar Qur'anic inscriptions.

The tarmac ended. The road continued along a dirt track which led into untended dry grass fields. I had found the graveyard Akram wished me to see, the place where Ayatollah Khomeini's agents disposed of their political enemies.

Scorched patches marked the spots of recent fires. Rubbish piles had accumulated in lumps over the sandy fields. Large macabre crows hopped about ominously calling to one another. Overgrown grass twisted over broken rectangles of badly poured cement, anonymous grey shapes resentfully marking the graves of a deliberately forgotten people.

Thirty-five lashes a bottle

Isfahan, Iran
September 29

I arrived in Isfahan by late afternoon. My hotel had undergone a recent trauma. A Spanish backpacker, the recent celebrity Rafael, had risen to fame after US$2,000 dollars had been stolen from his room. The surprisingly efficient Isfahan police had found the culprit within two days. The previously convicted criminal had paid for a room only to set about making keys for other rooms. This way he had succeeded in ransacking tourists' luggage. He had relieved the unfortunate Rafael of all his money, his entire budget for his prospective journey all the way to Nepal. An efficient German cautioned me on the staircase. 'Zis is not a safe hotel. You must put ze valuables in ze hotel safe.' It felt more like an order than a warning.

I was given the keys to a room already part-occupied by a small Japanese man, Dr Youshi, a recently graduated medical student. He appeared not to place particular importance on his studies, as he sat on his bed chain-smoking cheap Iranian cigarettes. That evening we ventured out together. The busy night time streets were crowded with large Iranian families who shopped, smoked and queued for banana milkshakes.

Isfahan was a desert city, comfortably blessed by the Zayandeh River, an oasis in the barren dry landscape. She was famous for her historical bridges. We reached the waters of the Zayandeh River and found the Si-o-Se bridge, which is constructed across the river like a carpet of small beige bricks. The bridge acted as a favourite promenade for Isfahanis, who walked up and down the main walkway chatting together. People swarmed the bridge's banks that lead down to a stone path that ran under the bridge on her jutting foundations. Waterfront cafes were balanced on steel sheets interconnecting the huge stone foundations. Water flowed underfoot as young and old bubbled away from water pipes. The café owners had plastered their arches with a miscellany of junk. Antique lamp shades, swords, pictures, drapes and door tassels hung off dusty pegs. Entrepreneurial teenagers rushed back and forth shouting orders to the sweaty old men who had been consigned to the worst job: sorting out and assembling the various flavoured tobaccos. They perspired furiously digging into the red hot furnace of coal pieces. Long metal pincers were used carefully to place glowing charcoal onto tobacco cups which slowly cracked under the heat.

Dr Youshi switched from his cigarettes to a cool menthol water pipe. He had found a deserted room dug into the walls of the bridge's foundations. We ducked our heads into the carpet-covered room surrounded by plush pillows where we sat staring out at the gliding river. Powerful pumps sprayed tall jets of water into the air. The glistening vapour from the jets vibrantly reflected an array of colours that shone from revolving lights placed under the pumps.

My lack of any Japanese meant we conversed in simple English. Before long our conversation had dried up. Dr Youshi abruptly moved out of the room and went to sit on a bench by one of the many tables outside. Reluctantly, I joined him.

Uninvited, a stooped figure in a white shirt with a carefully trimmed beard, sat down on the end of the bench. He introducing himself as Sevak, an Armenian Christian, and quickly jumped at the chance to speak English. Sevak turned out to be a Tehranian who had come back to Isfahan for a family funeral. He told me of his aspirations to travel to America for work, although he had recently had a set back in his application process. I groaned internally, predicting the usual questions of 'Can you get me a visa for Britain?' and other impossible tasks which so many seemed to ask from me.

However, my fears were unfounded as Sevak explained his plight. He hoped to join his family who were already in America. He had an interview in Frankfurt the next morning, which he was unable to attend as his passport had expired and it took four months to process the application for a new one. Therefore he had missed his slot with the US immigration department.

He soon spoke of the Christian Armenian community in Isfahan and the difficulties he had run into whilst transporting illegal bottles of wine. Budhra had told me about the Armenians of Isfahan being local illegal producers of alcohol for the domestic market. Sevak told me he was not involved in that illicit business, although like many Christians he too occasionally enjoyed a drink.

'My sister had made me two bottles of red wine, which I was carrying in a plastic bag. I was walking past a policeman and he saw the bottles and asked me what they were. I lied, but he did not believe me and opened them. He found out they were wine ... I went to court and they ordered seventy lashes ... But because I am a Christian the police were more lenient with me. I had the full seventy lashes but I was fully clothed with a bible under my arm ... I was lucky. There were eight young Muslims with me who had been joking about drinking again and how much fun it was. The flogger whipped them with no clothes. Although they each received only ten lashes, the sounds of their screaming were terrible. Their backs were covered in blood.'

* * *

The next morning, Sevak offered to show me 'New Jolfa', the Armenian district of Isfahan on the south banks of the Zayandeh river. Sevak told me about his community's great exodus from Armenia after the great Safavid ruler, Shah Abbas I, had pursued a scorched earth policy in order to protect his northwestern frontier against Ottoman advances. In 1618, the Safavid ruler tolerantly signed a decree granting land south of the Zayandeh river to 150,000 displaced Armenians. After a gruelling journey in which many of the Armenians perished, the Shah of Persia rewarded the community with religious freedom, interest-free loans and the unheard of liberty of electing their own mayor.

It was immediately apparent that New Jolfa was different from the rest of Isfahan.

Over twenty churches and the larger community's houses had been condensed into a stretch less than 3 km long. On entering a church, small rectangular doors had been cut out of larger arched doors forcing all to bow before God. Despite

The Great Theatre, Ephusus, Turkey

Karim Khan Avenue, Tehran, Iran

Behest-e-Reza Cememtry, heading out to the forgotten fields,
Mashad, Iran

A Zoroastrian Tower of Silence (Dakhma), where the dead
are left to decompose, Yazd, Iran

Dhows, Ras Al-Jinz, Oman

16th century mud brick tower house,
Shibam, Hadramaut, Yemen

Rural, armed Yemenis amused by my phtographic efforts, on the road from Al-Hawf to Al-Mukalla, Yemen

Ghat market, Old City, San'aa, Yemen

St Catherine's Monastery, Sinai Peninsula, Egypt

'Zorba' (Kyriokas) in typical fashion, St Catherine's
Monastery, Sinai, Egypt

An Upper Egypt Sai'idi, wearing his Galabia steering a felucca up the Nile from Aswan, Egypt

View from the Old Cataract Hotel where Agatha Christie wrote 'Death on the Nile' Aswan, Egypt

St Georges Hotel, after the bomb blast that killed Lebanese
PM Rafiq Al-Hariri, Beirut, Lebanon

Place De Martyrs' Cedar Revolution camp, Beirut, Lebanon

View from Shatilla, the infamous Palestinian refugee camp, Beirut, Lebanon

Entering Ramalla, the West Bank, Palestine

Shah Abbas's famously open-minded approach to governance, he had insisted that the churches had a mosque-styled dome. However, instead of the Muslim crescent moon, crosses poked out from the mud-baked domes.

Inside the churches, rich paintings covered entire walls depicting individual New Testament scenes, a once useful visual aid for illiterate congregations. Only St Jacob's church broke from the traditional dark decor, with simple white walls that curved into hollow arches, with bright blue edges highlighting her architectural symmetry.

Sevak was adamant that we should visit the centre for Armenian Christianity within Iran, Vank Cathedral, the seat of the Ecclesiastical Council of Gregorian Armenian Christians, named after St Gregory the Illuminator who converted pagan Armenians to Christianity in 301 AD. The cathedral had just received a new bishop from Beirut, news that had sparked enormous excitement among the community of New Jolfa.

The cathedral was a sharp contrast to my Church of England stereotyped ideas of what a cathedral should be. The Armenians had ignored high ceilings and stylized crafted stone work. The cathedral dome rose like a buoyant onion into the blue sky. Inside biblical illustrations were squashed into one metre square boxes around the walls. Each image was divided by golden floral shapes that twisted to the ground. The dome itself acted as a canvas for blue and gold drawings of a winged face whose symbolism I never understood. The face was that of a seraphic girl who appeared from four imposed corners around the circular dome. The girl was bodiless with wings that sprouted from behind her ears. Each corner was dominated by one large face with two smaller faces flying beneath.

The cathedral also had some harrowing images. One wall

had been entirely devoted to a triple-decker painting of heaven, earth and hell. Those in heaven knelt in solemn prayer, all facing inwards towards God on his divine cloud. One level down, the mere mortals paraded around in united marches. Hell was a land of naked bodies screaming in pain, as spears from every angle punctured soft flesh creating wounds from which blood gushed. A dog similar to my idea of the 'Hound of the Baskervilles' rose up with spikey teeth to feed on the lost souls.

Back outside, Sevak was eager for me to join him at a four-pronged statue in the centre of the square. The plaque read 'The Martyr's Monument' marking the 1915 Armenian genocide, when the perishing Ottoman Empire decided to cleanse her Armenian subjects in the final moments of her regional autonomy, the Armenians' own holocaust. This unremarkable statue did little to explain the genocide. The museum better illustrated the true horror. A huge map of Turkey flashed with red lights, marking the sites where the many massacres had taken place. A video had been set to repeat, flashing images of starving children and mass graves. Displayed behind a glass case sat a monstrous document, the cable from the then Minister of the Interior and later the Grand Vizier, Mehmet Talat. His orders to the Governor of Aleppo were concise:

'As informed earlier than this, per orders of the Jamiat (council), the government has decided to exterminate the entire population of Armenians in Turkey.

The following cable reinforced his decree: 'Children, women and the sick will not be spared ... without listening to the voice of conscience, remove them all and put an end to their existence.'

Retribution followed in 1921 when joint Russian and British

Intelligence approval permitted the assassination of Mehmet Talat in Berlin, where he had fled after the fall of the Ottoman Empire. The assassin was Soghomon Tehlirianan, an Armenian genocide survivor.

The rest of the museum served as an Armenian bric-à-brac warehouse. The press room boasted of having been the first establishment in the Middle East to print The Book of Psalms in 1638. The last used printer was a giant black machine from London, made by Clymer and Dixon, whose handle sprouted into a double-headed eagle that the publishers would have twisted and turned to bring about the printed form.

Passing traditional clothes and bibles of all colours and sizes, I came to an extraordinary display dedicated to the skills of a very adroit man. In 1974, an Armenian from Tehran had inscribed the first Armenian proverbs of Vahram Hakopian, onto a human hair, less than 0.1 mm thick using a diamond-tipped pen. He had written:

To know wisdom and instruction,
To perceive the words of understanding.

Inside the library, a rare sight of unveiled women set out a spread of Armenian newspapers which emphasised the spread of the diaspora with bound copies from Syria, Lebanon, Australia, Iran and America.

Propped up against the walls, sat the first Armenian global map from 1695. Topographers had an overgenerous view of North Africa and Sub-Saharan Africa before snaking down to a vertical tail from the Congo to modern day South Africa.

* * *

For an Armenian explorer of this century, Sevak took me to meet his father, Lernik. We entered a courtyard with a lonely fig tree that provided shade to the balcony above. The house was classically geriatric. Dust had conquered every surface, covering a hoarded treasure of old newspapers, books, rickety beds and children's toys sitting in piles in abandoned rooms. Sevak shrugged in capitulation. 'I have tried to clean this place, but my father insists on keeping everything and my father hates cleaners. He says they disturb his peace.'

Climbing down the steps to the courtyard below, Sevak appeared from the kitchen with a tray of fruit and Turkish coffee. We sat under the fig tree watching ants crawl up the trunk. The front door opened loudly as Lernik hobbled in, thrusting his walking stick and coat aside to introduce himself in fluent English. He sat in Sevak's chair and sharply ordered his son to fetch more coffee from the grubby kitchen.

'It is nice to speak English again after so long. I have been to England, you know. I have written three travel books in Armenian about my trips to Europe, America and finally Armenia.' Lernik turned to Sevak and spoke some imperatives. Sevak was a dutiful sherpa and scurried into the house to fetch his father's books. He reappeared with three hardbacks filled with black and white images of the 1960s.

During his life, he had made such a significant contribution to Armenian academia that Cambridge University had awarded him an honorary diploma which hung proudly on the wall. The old academic was modest in his accomplishments, and instead stood up and beckoned me to follow him. 'Come and see my souvenirs from my travels.'

We walked back into the house and past the mounds of archives to a table displaying a small Eiffel tower, a metal plate of Australia, a New York snow globe and a little puppet guardsman.

'This one's for you,' he said smiling.

Sleeping Carlos and the Greeks

Sinai, Egypt
March 17–20

Our small group of tourists awoke to the freezing night air of Sinai at 2.15 am. Alex, an English plumber, Tom, a Dutch computer engineer, an annoying Japanese girl whose profession I hadn't discovered, and I, packed our bags and left the dingy hotel. We set off along a dirt road which coursed its way towards the start of the trail up Mount Sinai.

Thirty large buses groaned along the tarmac road. Their cargo of sleepy tourists reluctantly descended from slumber. Their faces told of a desire to return to the Intercontinental Hotel, BBC World Service and bed. A few wooden shacks marked the entrance to the trail, their owners eagerly selling the most expensive bottled water on the African continent, as well as poorly made, Arafat-like, acrylic headscarves. A line of policeman marked the entrance, arms outstretched making apathetic bag searches. Our happy group resembled Michelin men as we wore all our clothes against the cold. The foursome broke formation as we walked past the first dozen tented restaurants and snack stops. Dubious Bedouins called out their well-rehearsed lines, 'Please come in. Bedouin hospitality – you don't have to buy anything, come and have a rest.' Gullible prey fell victim to the calls and sat momentarily on grubby benches before the carnivores descended with trays of confectionery. If unwilling to conform, a few English expletives would mark the tourist's departure onwards for the next jaunt on the ever increasing mountain gradient.

Our climbing compatriots ranged from the more serious amblers bulging with 'North Face' clothing and ridiculous telescopic sticks designed for Everest base camp, to ancient grannies who, out of pure conviction, moved slowly up the mountain. Three Russian girls in their mid-twenties were an eye-catching sight as they overtook our group. They ambled along unfazed by the cold, wearing high-heeled shoes, clutching handbags, flaunting tight 'Miss Sixty' jeans and skimpy, cleavage-hugging tops.

The path to the summit of Mount Sinai was shown by a long tail of lights that snaked uphill, making hairpin turns every four hundred metres. After walking for two hours, the path curved around the back of the mountain to the appropriately named stone staircase, the 'Steps of Repentance' with its seven hundred and fifty stairs.

The walled summit spread out into an irregular courtyard with two square buildings, a church and a mosque, set against the backdrop of an orange, glowing Sinai. The mountains across the peninsula cut up into the sky. Their jagged edges, rough like uncut diamonds, peered out from the cold darkness.

The Russian girls were part of a larger Russian Orthodox group. They formed a circle of small candles, praying at the point where Moses received the Ten Commandments.

As the dawn ascended, the same orange glow spread down the valley we had just climbed through. The corner of St Catherine's Monastery appeared in the morning light, creeping into view from behind the mountainside. Behind the high wall that enclosed the monastery's square base, a dense plethora of buildings rose up at various angles and heights. The acrid smell of 'Cleopatra Lights' cigarettes hung down the path from resting Bedouin, watching the cash train descend. Their camels knelt in the dust, necks extended, slowly turning like snakes looking around for more entertaining sights than their masters.

Outside the monastery, a single door marked the entrance and exit for opposing lanes of human traffic. Inside, groups gawped at the not so truthful 'burning bush' which had recovered in the last thousand years from a previously charred appearance, and now burgeoned in a corner like a green mop with Rastafarian shoots.

I was particularly interested to make contact with one of the Greek Orthodox monks who inhabited St Catherine's. Back in England, during the dark days of A-levels, the Blundell's school chaplain had told me about one of his past pupils, the then schoolboy Nick Webber and now monk Father Nilus. Despite two letters from England, I had not managed to make contact with Father Nilus. I asked a surprised Egyptian boy, *Salem*, if he knew the monk? Nodding in response, I handed him a small message before he scampered off to find Father Nilus, who soon appeared strolling down a path from the 527 AD Byzantine basilica.

Father Nilus was an impressive sight with his heavy black beard, vertically peaked black cloth hat, a holed black cardigan, and the standard black cloak that fell down to his feet. He welcomed me to the monastery, before we exchanged references to Blundell's and I apologised for my unannounced arrival despite my prior attempts to make contact, defending its abruptness due to the Egyptian postal service.

Father Nilus stopped his morning commitments and led Alex, Tom and I (the Japanese woman had thankfully returned to the hotel) through a museum of small, pokey rooms, each specialising in a particular theme. Electric lights lit stone walls, covered with icons which had survived the Byzantine emperor, Leo III's iconoclast demands in 726 AD, due to the monastery's remoteness.

The golden paint of the icons glimmered behind glass frames and cabinets. All the icons in the first room followed a scene essentially sacred to St Catherine's, depicting Moses standing before the burning bush, receiving the Law of God.

Despite their age, the icons remained well preserved. It was possible to make out an artist's tiny brush strokes painted in the sixth century. Father Nilus drew our attention to one icon in particular, an image of St Peter. The icon was, for Father Nilus, 'full of symbolism' as he pointed out the religious meanings within the ancient painting. With his large ears, St Peter was a listener. A small mouth symbolised the saint was a man who held his tongue, whilst in his hands he clutched the three keys to the Kingdom of Heaven.

Though not an icon, one golden painting recorded all the monks who had lived in St Catherine's during the second half of the eleventh century. The painting hung in two hinged halves, in the shape of a loaf of bread. Each side had eight rows, each row containing twenty-three sets of three people, about 552 people per side. What was remarkable was the individual depiction of each man, whose detailed face and outline could distinguish him from his colleagues. Tiny red writing in Greek under their feet stated the name of each monk, every man an individual among the collective whole.

The museum displayed other, more swiftly produced pictures. Lovely black and white photos from the 1868 Ordnance Survey of Sinai hung along the passage into the second room.

The second room housed the monastery's Who's Who/visitors' book. The room listed chronologically almost everyone who had visited St Catherine's whilst in power. The secret to the monastery's longevity lay in its successive acquittals from the rulers of the era. In 1798, it was Napoleon's turn. He personally signed a decree of protection to the monastery, and for the freedom of travel to the monks. Marianne, France's national emblem sat heroically, wearing the odd-looking Father Christmas-like droopy hat, a spear in hand, with the calligraphied words: 'Voulant favorir le Couvent de Mont Sinai' (Those that favour the covenant of Mount Sinai).

Sadly, Napoleon's generosity was eclipsed by a man with a far greater entourage; even a prophet had granted immunity to the monastery. Before Mohammed had established Islam, he had been running camel-trading caravans through the peninsula. The monks of St Catherine's were said to have felt the power of God from Mohammed. The Prophet of Islam returned in the second year of the Hijrah having fled Mecca for Medina. He bestowed his blessings upon the monastery in a dispensation, protecting the rights and privileges of the monks and granting their exemption from military service or taxes. Despite speculation as to the whereabouts of the original document, the monastery possesses a number of copies of the charter as the original was reportedly taken to Constantinople and never returned after the Ottoman conquests of Egypt in the time of Selim I in 1517. The copy on display was written in Turkish under the Arabic script. The bottom left of the page bore the outline drawing of an enormous hand, supposedly, though unlikely, that of Mohammed.

On the other side of the room, gold and silver twinkled in a display of ecclesiastical gifts to the monastery from various foreign dignitaries. The monastery's wealth seemed to comprise an inordinate amount of functionless, golden trinkets from the Kremlin, Lebanon, Cyprus, Crete, Bucharest, Palestine, Venice and even as far afield as Calcutta.

As the final tourists were leaving, Father Nilus asked where I was staying. On hearing of the hotel down in valley, he offered me a room in the monastery for a few days. I was excited to have been allowed into the inner sanctum. The old Blundellian led me past the departing tourists and through gates marked 'Private' to a small room where another monk sat on duty guarding a desk. He leant back on his chair and poked his hand into a wooden box of keys. I was led up to the northern wall. A wooden balcony ran across the front of the monastery's spare cells. Father Nilus pushed 'Room 14' open. 'I am afraid you may find it a little basic?' he warned me.

Room 14 was far from basic. It lacked the nocturnal delights of cockroaches and bed bugs, the main features of the sort of cheap hotels to which I had grown accustomed.

Next door was a kitchen where I learnt to make Turkish coffee before beguiling the afternoons away, peering over the balcony's wooden railings looking down on the monastery below, covertly finishing off *Operation Desert Storm and Instant Thunder* by General Norman Schwarzkopf, an inappropriate read at odds with this place of peace.

From my vantage point, I could gaze across the monastery to the opposite wall. Similar to the side of my cell, the wall rose up at an angle of 15–20 degrees, following the sloping mountain gradient. The western wall peered over the others, standing boldly as the newest and largest development. The wall acted as the back bone for a new development of cells. A central staircase divided the cells on four floors. The facades were smeared with a lick of earthy brown paint.

Every morning, the eastern wall held out the army of tourists during their dawn attack. Yet it was possible to see the defensive adjustments which had been made to the monastery; smaller stone blocks had been added to the eastern wall, layering over larger Justinian slabs in attempts to raise the height of the defences against sniper fire after the introduction of rifles.

Despite the museum's treasure and implied wealth, the monastery was in need of some restoration. One small room of mud and straw edged out, sagging dangerously off the eastern wall.

One of the simplest joys was to look out over the monastery's hedgehog spikes of buildings, which like skewers, punctured into the sky in a multitude of sizes, shapes and angles.

After I had settled in and Father Nilus had finished his morning job of preparing lunch with his Bedouin chefs, we sat down in the shade as the bustle and chatter of tourists ceased. The monastery returned to silence and tranquillity once more.

Sitting on the other side of the table from Father Nilus, I joked that, in the world of the monastic orders, Father Nilus had reached Ivy League heights. He told me of his youth. Having studied psychology in North London he had become increasingly interested in Christianity and God. 'But, I was driven here by God's providence. I came to visit one day, just as you are now. Soon days turned to weeks, weeks to months, and I was asked if I wanted to stay.' Twelve years had passed since that first day.

We spoke of faith in an academic capacity as I was, and remain, an enthusiastic agnostic. Recalling my A-Level theology I asked him his opinion of a moral atheist in the afterlife. At this point, without introduction or invitation an energetic face appeared, as a Zorba-like figure came swaggering around the corner. He was a short, thin man, greying slightly, though ebullient at the sight of a new face. I could almost hear the Sirtaki soundtrack following in his wake. Clad in jeans and a T-shirt, this was clearly no monk. Smiling mischievously, he pulled up a chair, seizing the opportunity to persecute Father Nilus. Having overheard our discussion, he independently answered my question.

'I think when we all get there we are met at a large door. Someone then shouts, 'Hey, Jesus, or Mohammed, this one's for you!'

Father Nilus smiled politely before giving his answer that all would be given a sign of God. Initially, we should have faith before God's presence would be revealed to us.

The war-mongering Greek was soon bored by this explanation. With an impish smile he continued his wind up. 'Zorba' waged war on the subject of the 'corrupt clergy': 'Just look at Greece, and look here!' gesturing to Father Nilus. 'They are all well-fed, hardly a life of poverty.'

He was remarkably disrespectful, added to which he was obviously a guest. Father Nilus was a gentle man and did not seem to know how to deal with these antagonistic comments. He soon departed for prayer, I thought, on account of Zorba's presence.

Zorba remained and without his audience, he calmed down and introduced himself as Kyriakos. He was a Greek artist from Hellas and was staying at the monastery to work, rather than play the act of an unwanted court jester.

Daily at one, monks and guests alike met for lunch in the refectory. Father Nilus led me through the monastery's labyrinth of staircases, balconies and paths which mingled between the many buildings. Taking a small diversion, we stopped off at the monastery mosque. A white, plain minaret had stuck out from right under my nose when I had sat on the balcony outside my room. Not paying attention, I had missed it altogether. It was a simple building, sandy coloured with wooden doors and wooden screen windows. Peering through the shutters, I could see in the poor light a clean, unused, white interior. From the middle of each arch swung lonely lamps. A dusty Qur'an stand revealed the building's redundancy, a mosque built by necessity rather than choice. As Father Nilus explained:

'Hakim Fatimid, the Caliph of Egypt came at the beginning of the tenth century. He thought himself to be God's representative on earth due to his descendancy from Fatimid, Mohammed's daughter. When he came to the monastery he saw Mohammed's decree pardoning the monastery. Because of that, he didn't destroy the monastery but insisted that a mosque be built. There is a good reference to the mosque from an eighteenth century explorer. He wrote about a mad goat that manically guarded the mosque's entrance.'

Sadly, the mosque was obsolete, as it had not been built to required standards and did not point in the direction of Mecca. However, the mosque highlighted a point I often overlooked, the closeness of Judaism, Christianity, Islam and the kinship of prophets. The three Abrahamic faiths collectively vouch for the story of Moses and the revelation of the Ten Commandments on Mount Sinai.

Continuing our walk to the refectory, Father Nilus commented on the fasting period in the run up to Easter. (Regrettably for me, this dictated daily trips outside the monastery to seek out ridiculously priced Mars bars from the Egyptian 'restaurateurs'.) But it was an important period for Father Nilus. He supervised the Bedouin servants in their preparation of the monks' diet. My hunger pangs made it hard to summon up enthusiasm on hearing that dairy products, oil and meats, which according to Father Nilus 'heighten the desires,' were temporarily unlawful.

The refectory was a rectangular building whose walls and ceilings curve inwards in the shape of a boat's hull, with a central arch running from either end. We were late and entered to a silent scene of black-clad figures listening to the white-bearded Father Parlos, the Diacasion (second-in-command) reading aloud in Greek from an Orthodox bible. Meals were not a social occasion. Each man sat accumulating nourishment on his plate in mounds of hot vegetables and bread with bowls of risotto or soup. Surrounded by contemplative diners coupled with a linguistic barrier, I had ample time to examine the refectory between mouthfuls. We sat around an eighteenth century table, with long borders on either side and loosely fitted drawers, that acted as the platform for piles of plates and ladles collected around a huge soup cauldron. The table legs ran to the floor with dusty carvings of lions and unicorn signets. Egyptian wine under a French label, sat unloved in plastic gallon demi-johns, their levels remaining unaltered due to festive restrictions.

Outside the refectory, a small cusp had been sketched out in the building's stone door frame. Father Nilus casually commented on it, 'Oh, the refectory used to be a Crusader barracks. That's where they would sharpen their swords.'

On my first evening, Father Nilus took me up to the top floor along the western wall where Father Justin, an American monk, was showing some friends from Cairo, the monastery's library. In my mind, Father Justin had unwittingly won the monastery's 'most memorable beard competition'. He had a great, greying hirsute hedge that ran from his moustache, over the precipice of his mouth to unite with a central gauze falling from his chin.

We entered the library to the wonderful scent of academia, that slightly damp and stale smell of knowledge that antiquities often exude. The room was filled with books of brown and crinkled edges and cracked spines. Father Justin started the tour by proudly announcing to his small audience that we were looking at the second largest collection of Greek theological manuscripts in the world, as well as a collection of additional manuscripts in thirteen other languages.

As well as books, a glass cabinet displayed the beautifully contorted calligraphy of the sixteenth century Ottoman Sultan, Suleyman the Magnificent's letter of protection to the monastery. Another case held a sixteenth century Persian history book, documenting Genghis Khan's obliteration of Asia; another, a colossal, gold ink inscribed gospel ordered by a twelfth century Byzantine king.

On the top of one glass cabinet, stood a framed letter from the British Library, asking the Archbishop, Father Danienos, to consider working with the library in re-piecing a very special copy of the Holy Scriptures, the **Codex Sinaiticus**, which dated back to the mid-fourth century. It is one of the fifty copies produced by Bishop Eusebius of Caesarea (Palestine) for Constantine. These are thought to have been the first complete works of the whole of the Christian scriptures, the Old and New Testaments.

The monastery was lucky enough to have once possessed a complete copy which now remains fragmented across Europe.

The monastery's copy of the codex was stolen after Father Justin's predecessors had been duped by a German larcener who pilfered the codex after fifty-nine confidence-inspiring visits to the monastery. He vouched to return and instead fled with the valuable scripture to the Kingdom of Saxony in 1844.

The sleuth entrepreneur then divided and sold the manuscript in more profitable sections. One half was said to have gone to the Tsar, Alexander II, the other to the University of Leipzig.

The story moves into the twentieth century. The Russian monarch has been overthrown, and despite five year plans of industrialization and economic collectivization, 1933 saw the culmination of the Soviet famine and a dire need for fast money. The Kremlin found themselves being forced to sell their copy of the *Codex Sinaiticus* to the British Library.

Leaping ahead to the twenty-first century, the monks of St Catherine's wrote a stormy reply to the British Library demanding to know why they should work together, considering that the codex originally belonged to the monastery and should be returned to its lawful owners in true Christian spirit.

Underneath a photocopy of a *Sinaiticus* page, the monastery's angry text read: 'The monks of Sinai have never ceased in their justified request for the return of their Codex.'

Today, the codex lies in scattered segments around the world, the majority in London's British Library, some leaves in Leipzig University Library, a handful remaining in St Petersburg and some leaves in St Catherine's, recent findings after the renovation of the Towers of St George.

Despite the monastery's abstemious values, the library had not been deprived of a little extravagance. The techno-monk, Father Justin, showed us his new toy in a neighbouring room. He led us into a charged network of black power cables and Apple laptops side by side with Epson printers, all positioned around the room's centrepiece. As Father Justine explained:

'This is a special book cradle which was developed in Oxford's Bodleian Library. It has a rotating book rest so no pressure is placed on the actual spine. The book cradle is linked to a 75 million pixel camera which fires off 63 flashes per shot as each page is photographed, every page being turned by the machine. We then store the complete book on hard drive.' Portable yellow blocks of hardware used to store the immense flow of gigabytes, lay stacked in one corner, containing images for future reference.

Father Justin zoomed in on a small golden painting the size of a thumbnail. His 75 million pixel camera exposed the minutest of detail beyond the perception of the human eye. The whole Frankenstein contraption, with its cradles and pivots, sat encased in a thick, clear plastic box which stopped the fine Sinai sand from damaging Father Justin's £70,000 literature tool.

As the cold desert sky turned dark, the monks returned to their cells to sleep. The 4 am daily service stipulated early nights. A mountain breeze whistled through the church bell tower, violently flapping the monks' cloaks hanging on lines outside their cells. One by one cell lights flicked off. God's active worship was finished for the day.

* * *

Bedlam erupted that night. Alarm surged through the monastery, as Sergio, a Greek visitor, had not returned to the monastery. In the morning, monks, visitors and Egyptians chatted with worried faces. Chapel bells rang out reveille at three in the morning, announcing the start of the day and an hour for ablutions before the first chapel service.

I lay shivering in bed for the next forty-five minutes. All my ecclesiastical enthusiasm had gone. I stepped out into the howling darkness. The wooden floor and uneven steps creaked.

Inside the basilica chapel a row of wooden seats ran down either side of the aisle to a four-poster altar covered by a wooden, mother-of-pearl dome. A black velvet tablecloth had been spread across the altar which was covered in crosses and candles.

A few monks sat either side, cut off from one another by neck-high wooden screens. Within each seat, a wooden door, suspended on hinges, acted as a book rest should the congregation kneel.

Most monks chose to hide away in the chapel foyer or sneaked out of view, sitting either side of the altar. By the altar, a golden wood screen hung with window frames of saints. Younger monks and their seniors stood opposite each other reading passages in Greek from the Bible, occasionally breaking into song. A blue lampshade hung from the ceiling illuminating their large bibles.

It was a strange, cold, inspiring sight. The lack of sunlight meant that the blue lamps were the only source of illumination. As the morning progressed, chains hanging from the ceiling, loomed out from the darkness, each holding a regal chandelier or Tsarist donated *Kendilli* oil lamp. In the shape of wine goblets, they lay motionless in the air. On their chains, silver bands were wrapped around ostrich eggs to symbolise the resurrection.

Chandeliers' arms parted from bulbous silver shapes, sprouting four-headed eagles that branched out like chicks from a nest. As the sun gradually rose, the chandeliers' edges and curves slowly glinted in a silvery-blue light, their candle holders extending from the darkness like curled spiders' legs.

Despite the romantic descriptions, I started to lose my gaiety. There seemed no end in sight. Thankfully, others seemed to share my thoughts. I was encouraged to see monks rising from their seats for a quick break from the service, taking a short dawn walk. Others would simply have a social break and stand in the foyer chatting to one another, while lighting candles in a tray of sand.

Occasional processions broke the monotony as Father Justin walked up and down the aisle, swishing a silver thurible on a chain. The metal clinked with his rhythmic swaying as everyone dutifully stood as he passed by. The monks performed a custom every morning that I never fully understood. They would walk around the chapel, blowing some candles out, only to relight them a few minutes later.

Late attendees meekly edged in, stopping at the old Justinian doors. They knelt before the sixth century, fire-blackened, crusader-grafittied barriers. There they would perform the movements of the crucifix across their chest, before approaching and kissing a large bible.

On the first morning, I found courage and rushed away back to bed.

But later I used those cold mornings, before the exhausted hikers arrived, to explore the chapel. Pillars stood proudly on either side of the aisle. Three small chapels hid away within the Basilica's walls. Passing through saloon-like swing doors and green velvet covers, the archbishop would access the three altars. The Holy altar, behind a round apse, was sealed off by a floral screen of twisting vines and leaves. Nailed to a wooded cross and secured by thick chains above the altar, Jesus looked down on the congregation below. His cross conformed to the orthodox design, with three-prongs stabbing the air above Christ's head.

From the apse, the mosaic of the Transfiguration loomed above. Red scaffolding covered the earliest mosaics of the Eastern Church. Beyond the plastic sheets, Moses and Elijah stood with the three disciples, Peter, John and James, crouching at the feet of the Son of God.

At 9 o'clock, the chapel reopened for tourists. The religious stood with pens and paper, writing notes of prayers and lighting candles in the sand tray. Many wrote the names of bereaved or ill family and friends on cards before passing them to monks, asking:

'Please, Father! Pray for this man. He is at home, back in Germany and is very ill. We would be very grateful.' Smiling, the monks would take the notes and slip them inside their robes for evening prayers. Muslim tour guides would loudly herd their flock through the chapel, calling out 'Time to go!' in a list of European languages.

* * *

I awoke to find Kyriakos enjoying the excitement of the missing Sergio. He took delight in telling me of the latest events which I had missed while catching up on some sleep.

'They call you sleeping Carlos now. Everyone came into your room this morning, looking for Sergio, even the archbishop, while you just slept.'

I was worried that such slothful behaviour, and clear absenteeism from the 4 o'clock service would not be welcomed.

Although he was not the man to seek advice on what the monks thought, Kyriakos reassured me that it was all right.

He returned to the thrill of our fugitive's plight. Kyriakos imagined himself to be a detective, recalling Sergio's flight in a melodramatic voice before jumping to a completely unsubstantiated conclusion:

'Well, if he has gone to another place, another world even,' pause for dramatic effect, 'then it is his choice and it was meant to be.'

Together we had worked it out; Sergio was dead. After lamenting the loss of life, Kyriakos wished to expand his philosophy and ignore the obscurity of one individual. 'I shall not be worried or lonely. There are six billion people on this planet.'

He walked over to the small kitchen table where I sat with a cup of coffee, pulling a bag of pine nuts from his jacket pocket. In a second, he had forgotten the fallen Sergio. We had moved on to a temporarily Marxist line of thought.

'I believe in sharing. We must all share. I am not a selfish man, but, with pine nuts, well … they are all mine!' With that he scurried off to paint.

In the afternoons, after lunch and before the afternoon 4 o'clock service, the monks would fetch their small radios and sit outside on the monastery ramparts, often smoking or chatting on their latest Nokia camera phones. The monastery's flag, a merged 'A' and 'K' on a white cloth would flutter in the sun.

Looking up to Mount Sinai, or the mountains either side of the monastery, I often saw Kyriakos's easel. It was usually abandoned, perched on a rock among small crosses placed on the skyline.

* * *

I was to leave on the Thursday before Good Friday, but by chance, I saw the monastery's 'Christmas' presents arrive. It was not Christmas in truth, nor were the presents for the occasion. Every year, the Greek Government paid for a large haulage container to be transported across the Mediterranean from Athens to Port Said, and then driven onwards by lorry to the monastery, all with diplomatic immunity thereby denying the Egyptian taxman his plunder.

A great commotion of shouts from outside the monastery drew my attention to a freight lorry dropping off a chipped rusty, blue container. The local Bedouins who worked for the monastery, had parked a small pick-up truck next to the container's doors. In great excitement, they frantically carted off boxes.

Meanwhile, the monks had formed a happy circle inspecting their new goods, including gallons of Greek wine, a saviour from the foul Egyptian equivalent. All the gifts had come from the people of Greece, as well as the monks' own families. The excited crowd had soon created clouds of dust as the frenzy reached a crescendo. Eager monks stripped off their cloaks and, topless, joined the rugby scrum of bodies. Father Nilus stood at a distance patiently clicking on his digital camera.

The entire monastery had now appeared to witness the annual event. Monks emerged whom I had never seen. Despite its size and close proximity, individuals could hide way amongst the ant farm of different buildings, ramparts and staircases that divided the monastery into an impenetrable labyrinth. A new guest appeared who I also had not met. He was a sad looking, middle-aged man who walked around in jeans and a navy blue woollen jumper. He appeared to carry the burdens of the world on his shoulders as he lethargically stumbled about, surveying the logistical scene, speaking to no one.

On my fourth morning, all were relieved as rumours circulated that the departed Sergio had remained seasonal in his resurrection to face the Day of Judgment another time. I planned to take the 2 o'clock bus to the coastal town of Nuweibah before leaving Egypt to cross the Red Sea to Jordan's Gulf of Aqaba. I packed my belongings and went in search of Father Nilus in the refectory.

Kyriakos was already there. He hung around listlessly, shouting snippets of bohemian philosophies to an inattentive crowd. Father Nilus and his Bedouin chefs worked around him as the artist insisted on speaking whatever Egyptian Arabic he knew. On seeing me he smiled and beckoned me over.

'Hey, are you going today? Why? Stay! You can learn some Arabic. I have a great teacher.'

'Who's that then?' I replied.

'No, you don't understand. Everyone is my teacher. That is the beauty.'

Father Nilus entered, swinging a white dishcloth over his shoulder in resignation. Kyriakos was feeling a little more generous. He pointed to Father Nilus.

'He is the only one who makes noise.' He then pointed to me, 'and you, you also make noise and joke around. But I feel I don't understand my fellow Greeks. They have become monks and have decided to dump their childhood spirit. They've put it in a box and moved on. Sometimes I feel like an infant around them.'

With that, 'Zorba' said farewell and returned to his sketches above the burning bush.

The changing colours of a metaphorical taxi

Beirut, Lebanon
April 28

Diesel hung in the air at the grubby Charles Helon bus station. Lines of taxis patiently waited for customers departing to all destinations. I was on my way back to Damascus, and from there onwards through Jordan and across the border to Israel. Three of us sat waiting in the purple velvet interior of an old Cadillac. We still needed two more people before the driver would be happy to go.

'For God's sake!' an English-sounding man turned to me. 'You on for Damascus? ... OK, then, we'll go now. I can't be bothered to wait. I'll pay the extra fare.'

Ludwig Lloyd climbed into the front seat, leaning back smoking a cigarette as we pulled out heading towards the Syrian capital. Half German, half English, he was a university professor in Tripoli. Having completed his first degree at some 'dingy Welsh university', he confessed,

'I never worked. My father looked around for a degree course and only some grotty Welsh university gave me a place. It wasn't that bad. I'd pick up my work at the beginning of term and then came back to Germany.'

Ludwig was the sort of character you pray to meet on long journeys. We soon fell into more meaningful conversations other than Taffy polytechnics.

Ludwig described his life in Beirut during the civil war, a complex and in many ways unconventional war, where fighting would stop and start momentarily, and where different militia routinely swapped their territories and their alliances.

'The war was actually quite exciting. Life, sort of, went on. At the weekends you could fly out of Beirut very easily. The problem was getting back. That was far harder. Sometimes whole areas of the city would be stationary for days as fighting erupted. I remember once I was stuck in Julie Flint's apartment for five days (a Guardian reporter in Beirut 1983–90). We couldn't leave because of the shelling … and what did the useless embassy do? We called the British Ambassador, and he told us to watch BBC World Service, which would report on any changes in Lebanon. Generally travelling was far harder. I'll give you an example: this taxi ride from Beirut to Damascus cost US \$50,000 at the height of the war.'

I gasped in disbelief. 'You can't be serious?'

Ludwig nodded. 'Well, it was about the most dangerous drive in the world. Apart from being shelled or mortared, you had to cross between numerous militia checkpoints. The soldiers were fine if uniformed, but the scruffy teenagers were the worse. They could, and would, quite literally, do anything they wanted.'

Our Cadillac climbed the Eastern hills that tucked Beirut

into the coast. The hillside was peppered with hundreds of half-built, lonely villas.

'Urgh, who would ever want to live here?' Ludwig summed it up. Arriving during the civil war, Ludwig had known all the famous characters, Robert Fisk and even Brian Keenan, who had been down at the American University.

'Keenan? Christ he was bound to be taken hostage. He got a reputation for being loud. Getting drunk too often in the same bars. But, by God, he wrote a great book, completely off character. It's strange to think of him and McCarthy forming such a close relationship.'

Ludwig offered the driver another cigarette, and leant back to chat to the man next to me. The young Syrian man had sat silently for the whole drive. He showed us his Syrian passport, proudly stamped with an Australian work visa.

'I get married to an Australian girl. I fly Sydney next week.' He smiled from ear to ear. He would be leaving old Syria for what he considered a better, more lucrative life. Ludwig had a different opinion. He loved all things Syrian. When we got to the border, he jumped out of the car to the passport control uttering in relief:

'Civilisation, at last!'

I was confused. If anything I thought Lebanon had the airs and graces of civilisation. Ludwig looked amazed.

'Ha, Lebanon?! After all my years in Lebanon, I cannot tell you of one good Lebanese friend. They are rude and arrogant people.'

Syria also had some pretty unpleasant and 'uncivilised' individuals. The former president, Hafez Al-Assad, came to the top of my mind. His uncivilised nature was best shown when the city of Hama rose up in civil unrest in the spring of 1982 and the inhabitants announced their desire to form an

Islamic republic. Al-Assad's power had been directly challenged by the Muslim Brotherhood and in response, he bombed the place to pieces.

'What the hell's wrong with that? He wasn't the monster everyone thought him to be. He gave them three days to leave. They were directly challenging a secular state. Then he sent in the bombers ... Quite right. The last thing Syria needs is an Islamic republic.'

We moved on to less confrontational topics. Ludwig was interested in my travels. I told him about my route across Iran, into Yemen and up the Levantine to Syria. We agreed that Iraq would be an interesting place to visit, though not at the time of writing. Surprisingly, Ludwig had already been there.

'It was quite fascinating. I crossed into Kurdistan, although we were not allowed to call it that when inside Iraq. The British Foreign Office had given me a satchel of $60,000 US dollars. They wanted them delivered to some man in Iraq to pay the pensions of all the old British-Iraqi forces who had fought in the Second World War. Apparently, they were not pleased at the time to be fighting for the Brits, but I am sure the pension was welcome at a later date. Then I went to stay with a very entertaining lady, whose husband is now high up in the Iraqi government, no names! At that stage, she used to live in the beautiful countryside in Kurdistan. Cigarette hanging out of her mouth, she would wear jeans and T-shirts. She was a good laugh, a very amusing woman, of course a complete crook.'

I asked Ludwig in what way?

'Heavens, she stole loads of cash from all the charities. Nevertheless, it was all bloody good fun, travelling around the countryside, looking at the decrepit old Assyrian churches. It was a pity the ancient race of Christian Assyrians and the

Muslims had so many differences. The Muslims trashed all their lovely old churches. But I visited other minority groups during that trip to Iraq.'

Ludwig went on to tell me of his most memorable experience in Iraq, visiting the Yezidi. I had only once heard of the infamous 'Devil worshippers' before. Their notoriety stemmed from their worship of an angel created in the illumination of God, *Melek Taus*. For the Yezidi, it was *Melek Taus* himself, not God, who then went on to create Adam from dust. Subsequently, he disobeyed God by refusing to bow to his creation, Adam, advocating his superiority over Adam having been created in the illumination of God. God later praised *Melek Taus*'s disobedience and appointed him leader of the archangels.

Except for the happy ending with God's praise at this heresy, the story mirrors that of the Islamic spirit, *Jinn Iblis*. *Jinn Iblis*, as with *Melek Taus*, refused to bow to Adam. This led to *Jinn Iblis*'s banishment for eternity to Hell and the appellation of the name *Shaytan*, which in Arabic translates as The Devil. Such acute similarities between the two and other unorthodox Yezidi opinions, such as reincarnation and the more trivial prohibition of lettuce consumption, have resulted in the group's historic persecution.

Today, with a population of just over half a million, the Yezidi exist as a separate race, predominately living around Mosul, where they still suffer stigmatisation and violence at the hands of both Muslims and Christians.

'It was quite bizarre.' Ludwig continued 'When I went to their temple in Lalish, near Mosul, I received exactly the same tour as every bygone foreign visitor. My experience mirrored, literally word-for-word, accounts written by past travellers. Of course, I saw the famous towers, and, just as expected, they wouldn't let me enter their temple and go down a staircase to their sacred cave. I was told exactly the same words with which other foreigners have been brushed off. 'There is nothing there.'

* * *

Soon our taxi was approaching the outskirts of Damascus. After talking at length about the misunderstood Yezidi, Ludwig felt a need to reflect on the entrenched predominance and problems of religion in Lebanon and the larger Middle East.

'You'll find out soon enough that everything in this part of the world is centred around religion. People are starting to think, in this age of optimism, that Lebanon can become some cohesive nation of multiple faiths, living in harmony. Superficially, people are friendly towards each other across the street, but really as individuals, the Lebanese are defined by their religion. And religion is *the* factor in the Middle East that defines all else.'

We sat in silence passing drab streets. Rain droplets started to fall on the windscreen. It was not simply religion that upset Ludwig, he spoke again, this time on the stagnancy of the region.

'This car is a perfect example of what the Middle East is all about. As you know, Syria is not exactly popular with the Lebanese. Hence the Syrian army has recently pulled out of Lebanon. So this taxi driver, he is Syrian. But he has re-sprayed his car white to fit in with Beirut's taxis. ... Have a look when you get out, there's some chipped paint on the bumper. You can see it used to be red and yellow, like every other Syrian taxi. It's a classic. Typically in the Middle East, everyone paints over a problem. The primary colours remain underneath. Nothing really changes.'

Module 4:
An introduction to economics

Migration trends:
Bandar Abbas to Bangkok and back

Bander Abbas, Persian Gulf, Iran
October 11

As I walked down to the beach in Bandar Abbas, two lonely figures leant against the sides of a beached boat. The wide hull of the former car ferry had become embedded in the sand. She lay facing the bazaar, her front ramp folded down. A breeze block had been placed on the sand to act as a step for her two residents who had constructed an improvised tent. Driftwood provided a canopy frame for stitched hessian sacks and frail tarpaulin that flapped in the maritime breeze.

Further down the beach, concrete tables complete with seats had been shoddily built on top of a fast eroding sea wall. From the tables I could look down to the lapping waters below. Concrete steps descended from the sea wall, their angular contours showing signs of erosion commensurate with increasing proximity to the destructive waves.

At night, elderly entrepreneurs used these tables. Gas from the stoves blackened copper pots as dark flames licked up the sides of the bronze-coloured kettles. Flickering, the flames radiated kaleidoscopic colours through lines of awaiting sheeshas.

At dusk, I would sit and smoke through a variety of flavoured tobaccos. Great wafts of sweet tobacco twirled and floated away in front of a blue darkness that swept across the Persian Gulf. Shortly, tiny flickers of light would reveal the once hidden Hormuz Islands.

From my vantage point, I could look down to the lapping waves that occasionally permitted the last metal remnants of a scuppered hull to poke out of the water. Small crabs clung to the vessel's carcass, hunching together awaiting the next tsunami that splattered white foam over their resilient black shells.

I pondered on my impending departure to Dubai the following morning. I envisioned a cold lager, a cleansing shower and crisp bed sheets. My hallucinations were unwelcomingly disrupted by a tall Iranian man who sat down abruptly opposite me. He smiled under his prim moustache, announcing his arrival in perfect English before guessing my nationality.

'I am Reza, and you are an Englishman.'

'Yes,' I said.

'This is a rare sight in Bandar Abbas! You must be taking the boat tomorrow to Dubai.'

'Yes, I am.' Reza twitched with joy at his correct deductions.

'Good, you will like it there. It is clean and rich unlike this country. You see, I worked over in Dubai in a sweet factory. I lived there with my lady friend, earning money to send back home to my wife and children. But now I am back here and I can't leave because I am in trouble with the police'.

Reza was ostentatiously clandestine in his final words. It

seemed to be a deliberate ploy to entice me to ask why he was in trouble with the police?

So duly, I fulfilled his unspoken request. 'It's none of my business but, if you don't mind me asking, what did you do?' He looked pleased by my curiosity explaining his happy-go-lucky exploits.

'I am always in trouble with Immigration. I have tried to emigrate to a rich country before, legally you know, but it is very hard. So I was in Dubai and I was looking around down at the port. I saw a tanker with big containers marked 'Canada'. So, of course I thought it was going there.' He gesticulated with his hands anticipating my agreement.

'I went and bought lots of supplies for the trip. I called my family in Iran and kissed my lady friend goodbye. Then, I climbed quietly into the boat and hid among the cargo boxes for over a week. At last, the ship stopped moving. I came out from my hiding spot.' He stopped his story and looked at me with suspense. 'But we hadn't arrived in Canada, we were in Bangkok.'

Reza laughed loudly, mocking his logistical error. 'The boxes were owned by a Canadian shipping company but they were not going to Canada. Eventually the Iranian government paid for my flight back and it was all OK. I didn't even get into much trouble with the government.'

We ordered two more teas.

'Then, I got myself back to Dubai and carried on working in the sweet factory.' Reza clasped his hands under the table, rubbing his palms together. 'I was working illegally, but I was earning good money in Dubai, much more than I could ever earn here, in Iran. But still, I wanted a better life. I wanted to live abroad. So I did the same thing, but this time I found a boat going to Libya. Again, I hid and then sneaked out when we got to Tripoli.'

He sighed in reminiscence of his voyage. 'When I got to Libya I was happy. But the customs caught me and I was sent to some islands in the Mediterranean. I had to wait there for ages. It was very bad. I wasn't making any money. Again the Iranian government paid for me to fly back. This time they weren't so happy. Now, I have to stay in Iran for seven years and even then I might not be able to go back to Dubai. I am very sad. What about my lady friend there?'

Labour movement:
Dubai and the race-based economy

Dubai, United Arab Emirates
October 13

A gentle, competitive snobbery among expats was evident no
matter where I was in the Middle East. Their adopted country
was always vastly superior to that of their neighbours. Expats
in Oman relished their chorus of 'Dubai's sold its soul to the
West.' I agreed. There was little that was classically 'Arab' in
Dubai. But I loved it. For me, Dubai was a hazy dream world
of hedonism in the form of New Zealand steaks, Heineken
beer and DVDs.

One evening in late September, I boarded a shoddy ferry
brimming with Afghan refugees and Iranian workers to go
across the Persian Gulf from Iran's Bander Abbas to the Emirati
port of Sharjah. After a month in Iran, I was very happy to see
the reassuring signs of McDonald's golden arches and
Starbucks coffee.

A newly married English couple, the Wrights, gave me sanctuary. They had generously offered to have me to stay. I arrived in grimy clothes in a cloud of body odour as sweat dripped from my rucksack. I had become feral in the last two months as a lack of parental guidance and local conditions had forced concerns of personal hygiene to the back seat.

The Wrights lived in a luxurious villa near Jumeirah zoo. The zoo ran along the back road towards the enormous 'Mercato' shopping complex. In the evenings, I would clutch plastic bags and walk past the zoo's eagle cages to hear squabbling and squawks overhead. The birds of prey flittered about in their giant aviary. From their heights they peered down on the convoys of Ferraris, BMWs, Mercedes soft-tops that were standard issue, purring along Dubai's roads.

On my first evening, Mark took me on an expedition to Mercato before they flew back to London the next morning, leaving their house to the tender mercies of an eighteen year old. At the Mercato mall, Australians, Europeans, Americans and Brits sat in fat Starbucks coffee shop chairs, drinking cappuccinos at twenty times the price of their distant competitors across the Gulf in Iran. I was enamoured by the glossy, clean and white shine of the shops. I discovered a reawakened joy in the complacent knowledge of stacked shelves. At Hardees, KFC and Pizza Hut I could enjoy banquets for one followed by regular cinema visits to the complex's multiscreen facilities. Dubai was a near perfect mirage of western opulence and extravagance.

I found one clue that I was still in the Middle East. At Spinney's supermarket, I nervously entered the 'Pork shop'. I was nearly overcome with tears of joy. Muslims and Jews stood at the gates as, over-the-moon, I piled my basket high with bacon rashers, all the while imagining the burning, spitting fat which would give off the salty aroma of prohibition.

* * *

'The Arabs are the minority here by a long way,' started Mark, changing gear as we shot down the sea front from Jumeriah districts 1 to 5. At the time, there were only five Jumeirah districts which started with district 1 of chic villas and extended along the coast to the eyesore of district 5 that sprawled in a construction mess of anticipated high-rise hotels.

'All these hotels are for a predicted spurt of tourism. Dubai has a problem. Only 8 per cent of the economy is based on oil. Abu Dhabi, the capital Emirate further west, has all the cash. Thanks to the 'Father of Dubai' Sheik Rashid bin Saeed Al-Maktoum, Dubai has become a hub for trade and services. It's now the Wall Street of the Middle East. Global companies are opening offices here simply because everyone else is. It's an unstoppable vacuum.'

In the darkness of incomplete streets, we drove past the sunken foundations of hotels. In the pits of construction sites, an army of blue ants worked away in the high humidity under generator-powered floodlights.

Mark slowed down for a closer look. 'This is the four tier class system and these workers here are the lowest. At the top are the Emiratis, next Western businessmen, then Asian lawyers and accountants and finally the construction workers'. The poor labourers, both financially and circumstantially, slaved away in blue overalls, shifting steel cables around the future hotel's concrete foundations.

'If lucky, they'll get about US $400 a month for such work.

But the death rates on these sites are high. There aren't any laws or safety restrictions for these people. Just look up.' He pointed to the lattice foundations. 'There are no banisters or rails to protect these people falling from the top floors.'

I looked at these insect-like humans, milling about, performing an array of required tasks. Despite having been brought up in a country controlled by overzealous health and safety restrictions, it was hard to sit comfortably seeing this sharp end of capitalism. These men were the exploited, unrepresented masses, who worked for peanuts to build the future of a country that in turn had no concern for their welfare.

'Because of the heat and the overall exhaustion of the workers, the construction companies only really like to have labourers working for one year at a time. After that they are meant to be half as productive.' Hearing Mark's words, I visualised the Duracell bunny adverts, where, as with Dubai's blue collar workers, the pink drummer would expend all energy, keel over and be discarded.

After the Wrights had departed, I used the city's buses to move about Dubai. Everyday I would sit, as the token Caucasian, in the cold, air-conditioned buses that headed out of Jumeirah for the centre 'Bur Dubai'.

Looking out of the windows, other Europeans would drive past in their two distinctive groups. Porsches and Jaguars carrying the male bread winners, wound their way to the office. Following them, American GMC wagons and Range Rovers housed the school run of fighting children and stressed mothers.

In the morning bus trips, I saw the same downtrodden blue ants, who followed each other in centipede-like trails on bicycles. Two lines flowed in opposite directions. The night shift returned to Port Rashid and their squalid 'accommodation blocks', while the morning shift reluctantly peddled to the Jumeirah hotels as a traffic warden supervised the rare convergence of the Western office workers and the literally blue-collar labourers.

I sat in arctic comfort on the buses watching these scenes. On the other seats sat Mark's 'third group' in Dubai's economic hierarchy. My fellow travellers were the fully or semi-skilled subcontinent expatriates, Indians, Pakistanis, Bangladeshis, Chinese and Vietnamese. They ranged from nannies, house cleaners, maids and cooks at the lower end to the top echelons, mainly Asian men, of business service providers at hugely competitve prices. As Mark had earlier explained in greater detail,

'The problem is an Indian accountant gets paid a third of what you would pay a Brit to do the same job, and one is usually as good as the other.'

I questioned whether this was the result of pure prejudice or the varying costs of living in the UK versus India?

'A bit of both, but you're probably right, I am afraid. I've seen the way the Emiratis treat the Indians. They're not publicly insulting. It's just you can tell they don't respect an Indian or a Philipino, and that includes their judgement. The Arabs prefer to have Caucasians in all the key seats.' I wondered why Emirati judgements were so influential in the human resource departments of foreign companies in Dubai?

'Oh for any business venture, a foreign company needs an Arab 'sponsor'. A 'sponsor' will do very little. Perhaps he might send presents to fellow Arab 'sponsors' or use his *wasta*, that is his influence, to help one of his many companies in a predicament. However, that effort will be pretty minimal, and slap bang at the end of the financial year when everyone has worked hard, they'll come along and collect a good 50 per cent of the company's annual profits. That's why our Emirati neighbours across the street have an 18-year-old son who drives a Ferrari."

The Green agenda: One man's rubbish is another's treasure

Cairo, Egypt
March 5

Donkey carts creaked along uneven roads. Their cargo of refuse slid precariously from one side to another, occasionally spilling out over the side into the streets. Tower blocks of small red bricks distinguished themselves from the buildings of greater Cairo with 2 metre blue crosses on their outer walls. Above the crosses, blue lettering read, 'God is Love'.

Hosni drove slowly, fearful for his taxi. Entering Garbage city, we jerked along the streets, arching in and out of potholes. We had come to visit the 'Zabbaleen' the plural, active participle meaning 'The Scavengers.' As the descendants of migrants who arrived in Cairo in the 1950s, the Christian community has long been the established waste management solution to Cairo's daily tons of refuse.

With the aid of pigs, the Zabbaleen have provided a free

service in removing organic waste for their swine to eat, as well as collecting plastics and metals which they sort out before being sold as raw material scrap.

As we progressed along the streets it was easy to see the Zabbaleen's organised system at work, although the pigs remained concealed. Different areas had been allocated for different tasks. In one area, cobblers shredded treadless car tyres before using the rubber to reheel old shoes. In cubbyhole workshops, tucked away from the road, electricians pulled apart televisions and fridges, gleaning functioning parts before combining components in new electrical utilities. Next came the plumbers who carefully held roaring blow torches. They artfully fused random cuts of copper tubing together into some usable form of hardware.

Compared to these inconspicuous, modest tradesmen, the mechanics alone hogged the limelight. Bare soles poked out from under car chassis. Concurrent colleagues busily cut away at vehicle body works with metal grinders. Sparks flew out on to the streets where little children ducked under the golden rainbow. Older sisters followed, shouting at their younger siblings in an attempt to regain control during the brief absence of parental authority.

I was surprised not to see any children running up to the taxi windows with cheeky hands eager for baksheesh. Later I came to learn that the children of Egypt needed more than paper money alone. Pens, pencils and books were not supplied by government-run schools. With the average Egyptian monthly household income set at around £100 Egyptian (£10 sterling) a month, educational tools were a very distant second to food and shelter. The profits from gleaning scrap gave the entire community a purpose. This was a hive of activity involving all ages.

Surrounded by this great diversity of entrepreneurialism, one man sprung to mind, my opportunistic uncle. He would be ecstatic at the concentration of junk that had been accumulated in one area. Uncle James had one love outside his family other than his beloved Staffordshire bull terrier: car boots sales and profiteering from anything worn out and destined for a skip. Quite often, he would go out for a short dog walk and return hours later with a lead, no dog, but dragging a 1950s four rotor German lawnmower or suchlike. Here, as in the affluent Barnes car boot sales, a community had gathered to reuse, recycle and profit.

Like my uncle, the residents of Garbage City were not pretentious. They were not obsessed with the peppering of the adjective 'Green' or with verbs carrying the prefix 're-' in attempts to conform to political correctness. The Zabbaleen were the opposite of British 'Green' recycling communities as typified by liberal West Londoners looking out from sash windows with cups of 'Fair Trade' caffeine-free tea. The Christians of Garbage City followed their profession out of real poverty.

Hosni and I sat in a tea house with chairs and tables of rickety wooden cuts, secured by nails that had undoubtedly been plucked from previous employment. Garbage City and her occupants were unique in possessing both ingenuity and sorrow. This was real Egypt.

The pyramids of Giza or Abu Simbel were not representative of this Egypt. They belonged to an ancient time thrust into the twenty-first century for the enjoyment of foreigners. Over four thousand years later and away from budget holiday hysteria, the Zabbaleen of Garbage City were a case that captured the imagination of many. But they were no different from the majority of modern day Egyptians, confronting the same challenges over insurmountable odds.

Life in Egypt was queuing for government-subsidised bread. Life was remaining single as underemployed and underpaid young men struggled to buy flats to attract potential wives. Life was nepotism and stagnation. Life was largely predestined and inflexible. Life was hard.

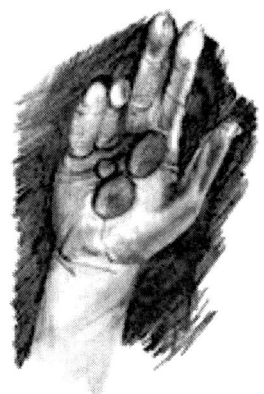

Economic inequality: The guilt of giving

Aden bus station, Aden, Yemen
December 20

It was time to leave the colonial port of Aden. I sat in the bus station waiting room. My host's driver returned with a negotiated bus ticket that would take me up to Sana'a, Yemen's capital city.

Outside I could hear a gas stove heating a hissing, boiling pot of water. Taxi drivers had formed semi-circles in conversation over scalding tea.

A small figure appeared at the door. A little African face pressed up against the glass reconnoitring the inmates of the waiting room. Cautiously, he opened the door. He almost tiptoed to my seat wearing ripped shorts and a grime-encrusted T-shirt, frayed at the small sleeves. He changed course and sat a few seats away from me.

I pretended not to notice his presence and continued slowly reading my book. Every word seemed meaningless as my mind was unconcerned by the dead letters.

Sorrowful, luminous eyes stared at me from an unmoving, sagging head. The little boy broke the stalemate pointing to my shoes with one hand and lifting a cracked plastic box filled with shoe polish and rags. I lifted my hand in an attempt to fuse refusal and gratitude.

The dramatic eyes continued their focus unfazed. He had all the time in the world. I did not. We both knew that I would eventually concede if he continued. It was only a question of when.

My conscience was being dissected. I myself, was the examiner, but the little boy set the standards. Together we concluded the inquest. I freed my mind from the weight of guilt for a few dollars.

His despondent face did not change as I knelt to undo my shoes. I passed them to him and felt an irritable annoyance when he did not seem eager enough to justify my defeated conscience. He diligently unpacked his tins and began to polish.

With the sound of brush against leather I returned to my book. I still read, but again I did not absorb the words. I felt a shameful euphoria from extracting my mind from the shackles of penitence.

After five minutes, he had finished. A last minute burst of kindness or was it guilt, saw me paying four dollars instead of the planned two. His face brightened momentarily. He bowed slightly and left.

His departure brought the second wind of self-induced shame. I sat feeling morally inadequate, reflecting on the array and extremes of thoughts that had occupied my mind in the last few minutes.

Minutes after the boy had departed, the door opened and a young African girl entered. With nothing to sell, she simply stuck out her hand. I feared the mental vortex again and handed her a note. She left.

Closing the door behind her, two figures loitered outside. Two black *abaya* gowns blew in the wind. The black outlines were further hidden behind the *niqab* mask that concealed eyes in a letter slip. The two harrowing figures looked through the glass door at me. The mendicant community had got wind of a cash-wielding 'Englistanee'.

My bus was soon to depart. I stood up to sling on my rucksack. The two door sentries noticed my movement and prepared their assault.

From the door, I could see the luxurious sanctuary of a white, modern Mercedes bus. In a confident manner, I flung the waiting room door open. Initially, I could not see my two adversaries. I made use of the advantage and weaved among restaurant tables in the direction of the bus.

Quite suddenly, the pair caught up with their fleeing prey. I was ambushed, either side, by the two swooping dark figures. I quickened my pace, ignoring my peripheral vision, eyes fixed on the haven of refuge.

With the change in speed, the two women kept pace behind me. They soon realised that my destination was fast approaching. Ten metres from the bus they took drastic action. I felt their rough leathery hands slowly gripping my wrist. Their grip strengthened with each step towards the bus.

The two were not going to accept my reluctance to give more. From behind their impersonal *niqabs*, yelps turned to shrieks and finally to wails as my feet started to climb the bus steps. Their howls brought a wave of emotions, culminating in an animalistic crescendo of despair and anger.

I slumped down on a back row seat and cowardly drew the curtain.

Module 5:

Sex and women's rights

Escaping sodomy

Tabriz, Iran
September 11

My clothes reeked of tobacco that had hung like smog in the carriage during my train journey from Turkey across the border to Tabriz, Iran. I was tired and hungry as I stood, irritated, surveying the shuttered bazaar. I had arrived without any Iranian Rial and, being a Friday, I was going to have to wait another day before cashing in some US dollars.

In Tabriz, I found that first appearances could be deceptive. When I arrived a seemingly kind old Azerbaijani hotel owner, Mr Letchiyn noticed my gloom. In attempts to boost morale, he communicated through the universal language of 'charades' explaining his wishes to show me around the town and 'El Goli Park'.

At El Goli, old men, students and soldiers kept a watchful eye over their children as they chattered away walking around the park's artificial pond. A black flotsam of nut shells had accrued on the pavement following the weekend hoards.

After buying two orange juice cartons, Mr Letchiyn fought for occupation of one of the heavily contested benches and murmured in broken charade-pidgin English and French his opinions on the beauty of his town. I agreed in sincere nods.

That same night, Mr Letchiyn proposed supper at his house. Apart from the small offering of orange juice, I had not eaten for twenty-four hours and subsequently accepted his offer with alacrity.

Half an hour after picking me up from his hotel, I sat innocently picking away at slices of watermelon in front of the BBC World Service. Mr Letchiyn held his hand above his head and wiggled his fingers in a frizzing action before pretending to dry himself. After his acting out a shower, he disappeared and had a real one. He returned looking refreshed. He sat down on the sofa and lit himself a cigarette, staring vacantly at the television.

It soon became apparent that Mr Letchiyn had British interests other than the BBC headlines, and without any prior hint that I had witnessed, he stood up and slowly unbuttoned his shirt and cast it away. His bulbous belly spilt out over his belt buckle. He smiled at me. I didn't smile back.

I could only think of the awful cliché that condoned all sorts of cultural relativist crimes when abroad: 'when in Rome', I had no interest in this local custom, only appalled horror. I imagined a plethora of unthinkable outcomes.

However, the strip tease had only just begun. Mr Letchiyn was without the need of a sleazy musical accompaniment. He either failed to gauge my lack of enthusiasm or simply didn't think it necessary for his performance. He went on to pluck off his socks, throwing the offerings on top of his shirt in a suggestive, casual manner. His pièce de résistance came as he unbuckled his belt and slowly unzipped his trousers. From the corner of my eye, I saw him looking at me as he kicked his trousers to the floor.

He looked to me for acknowledgement of his accomplishment. I was forced to turn and in that very English way, adopt the familiar, though unsure 'oh how funny' sort of face.

He sat back down on the sofa and finished his cigarette. I tried to ignore his advances. I fixed my gaze on the television screen. I soon thought it was quite possible that I too, could become a news item.

The insistent old man was quickly bored by my 'indifference'. He seemed to admire my coquettish 'hard to get' stance. He became even more determined and tried to attract my attention, calling 'Charlie! Charlie!'

Slowly I looked up to see him smiling, and insinuating with his hands that I too should join him in the casting off of clothes. At this juncture, all diplomacy disintegrated and I forcibly blocked his plans with meaningful hand gestures and a shaking head.

His plan was versatile. On meeting with failure, he quickly switched tactics. We entered a stage of role play. Mr Letchiyn was Alexander the Great. I was to play a lowly soldier being seduced by the victorious ruler in the Hanging Gardens of Babylon. Mr Letchiyn used his most effete Macedonian charm and lent forward to the table, taking a bunch of grapes from a glass bowl. He held the erotic food to his mouth and feasted away in dramatic, suggestive snapping head movements.

At that moment, I started to fear Mr Letchiyn. He shifted his body weight and pushed me deeper into my side of the sofa. He artfully plucked an individual grape and leant forward with an unassuming face. His hand wavered in the air before assuming its predesignated course, to my mouth. My body went rigid with muscles tensed in self defence. My hands shot up in protest. That was a big mistake. It only seemed to encourage him.

Again, he had another string to his bow. He placed the failed grapes to one side. The time of clandestine tactics was over. Mr Letchiyn concentrated his full force on one final attack. It was now total war. The tactician chose direct physical contact. Again, he retook previously held ground and moved over to my side of the sofa. A grey wrinkly hand edged out to no man's land. He reached up and tried to stroke the top of my head.

I evaded his foul fingers and stood up in protest. Looking back down on the sofa, I saw a dejected man. His face had lost the spark of optimism that seemed so promising a few hours earlier.

Still standing, I tapped at my watch before yawning in a Mr Bean like fashion. I ended the finale with a clasping of hands before raising them to my ear in a universal sleep gesture. The potential pederast shook his head in a menacing, omniscient way. He pointed at me with his index finger, reciprocated my sleeping gesture then pointed to the ground. After informing me that I was staying, Mr Letchiyn seemed reassured and happily retreated to his HQ, the bathroom, to draw up another plan.

The time was now. I retreated to the front door and checked my escape route. Thankfully, the key was still in the lock. I slowly turned the key and muffled the noise of the lock withdrawing. Edging the door open, I stepped outside. With one hand depressing the handle, I carefully shut the door behind me.

* * *

Once in Tehran, the infamous Budhra howled with laughter as I recounted the story. It seemed he hadn't heard anything so amusing in years.

He interspersed his booming chortle with snippets of wisdom. 'You should be warned, Charlie. You're a fair-skinned, blue-eyed young Englishman … ha! I can imagine many a man would quite happily pursue banditry with you.'

It was a strange compliment. I told Budhra all of the details, including the grapes and hair stroking. Budhra agreed. Mr Letchiyn's intentions were anything but proper.

'Charlie! Charlie! I know a story you can relate to. I have a friend who now teaches in England. He travelled on the famous 'hippy trail' all the way to Kathmandu in his youth. He first encountered problems in Istanbul when two Turks tried to lure him into sex. It happened again in Eastern Turkey. He was hitch hiking and the driver stopped the truck and they had a vodka party. The Turk tried to get him drunk so he'd give in … ah the Turks!' Budhra smiled from ear to ear recounting the story. Budhra's unfortunate friend was still to suffer further provocations.

'In Afghanistan, he was again hitch hiking. The Afghans were used to westerners on their hippy trail. The Afghans knew that more often than not, young tourists would trade sex for a lift. You see, the trail attracted lots of queers. But when my friend refused to be buggered, a huge Afghan lorry driver just picked him up and threw him in a river.' Budhra roared with laughter.

'He eventually got to Kathmandu, still a virgin in that sense, and guess who attacked him there? A gay British hippy.'

Budhra suppressed his sense of humour, adopting a more father-like persona to explain the dangers to me.

'The problem is that unmarried men cannot have sex with

women easily in these strictly religious countries like Iran and Afghanistan. So many teenage boys frequently have sex with each other. However, you must understand that many of these men do not consider themselves to be 'homosexual.' They think they are simply 'practising' sex. There is also a difference between the two people having sex. It is the man who is receiving intercourse that is considered to be homosexual ... but really, often men are like dogs. They don't care what it is.'

Sex and death in provincial Syria

Dayr as Zawr, Syria
April 5

As I got out of the taxi, I turned around to pay the driver. My cumbersome rucksack had gained momentum and crashed into a pyramid of carefully stacked aluminium boxes outside a shop. They crashed to the ground like dominoes with a great metallic clink. The shopkeeper gestured me towards him. Once in range, the unforgiving man smacked one of the fallen boxes into my chest.

On seeing the calamity, my taxi driver leaped out of the driver's seat and shouted in Arabic to pacify the aggressor. He turned to me and waved his hand, stipulating urgency, 'No problem. Do nothing, just go.' After finding my hotel, from then on I would dog leg around the box-throwing shopkeeper.

Down one back alley, I found a smart looking internet café. I sat and typed out a carefully edited version of events for friends and family. Unknown at the time, my future guide to the unofficial Syrian sex education syllabus sat on the next computer. The eager university student made loud efforts to attract my attention. He succeeded and quickly introduced himself as Ali. He seemed excited to be practising his English with a native speaker.

I told him my sob story of the tower of boxes. Ali was sympathetic. 'I hate it when they do this. If you were a Syrian, he would have done nothing. Sometimes people behave in this way because you are a foreigner and they think their actions are acceptable.'

We quickly formed a friendship. Over the next two days, Ali began to speak more openly and shared some sensitive information on his generation in Syria.

Ali was a welcomed guide. As a town, Dayr Az Zawr was a disappointment. Apart from the pea green twisting waters of the Euphrates, the place was a sprawling mass of dusty streets with characterless modern apartment blocks.

The most attractive element was the daily market which took place on the banks of the river and where rural famers came to town to sell their produce. Ali had a healthy apathy for 'these people' as he put it, people he considered to be ignorant as 'they don't want to study and instead they behave like animals in a most dishonourable way.'

A burly farmer barged past us on the pavement. He walked watching his footing, trying to avoid pools of blood, fat and intestines that stank in fermenting pot holes. His wife followed obsequiously, several paces behind. She was pretty in her black cloak. Golden jewellery clinked on her body. Ali did not see this beauty.

'That lady, she will not be able to read or write. But she does walk behind her husband, which I know, you think is strange, but here it is not. It is both good and bad.' He did not elaborate any further. Other farmers bellowed to each other from across the street. Ali winced as the men boisterously jeered and hugged each other.

Ali had two good friends. Mustapha was, as Ali introduced him to me, 'good looking and liked by all the girls at the university'. Apart from being the Casanova of the group, Ali explained, Mustapha was also the son of the local police chief.

'No one can say what they think of him. When I am angry with him, I have to be quiet. Here, in Syria, people's families matter a lot.'

Ali's second friend didn't have paternal immunity. Short and blithe, Talib looked like a docile sheep, but a friendly one. He was the youngest of the three and was teasingly nicknamed 'Kid' by the other two.

* * *

The four of us ventured out in Dayr Az Zawr and walked around aimlessly chatting amongst ourselves. On my first morning in Dayr Az Zawr, Ali arrived at my hotel to announce that we were all going to his local university. On hearing the news, I was rather apprehensive. It had been hard enough with just the three of them. They were polite and interesting but they had made me the centre of attention, something I had egotistically never objected to, but in Dayr Az Zawr I was a rare Englishman.

When walking down the street, the three would compete amongst themselves for my full attention. They would often lean across each other or walk directly in front of me so as to not be left out of the topic. Their three conversations erupted in a series of fast sentences before a rival could interrupt.

It was exhausting.

That morning we walked for half an hour out of town to their university. Once there, my discomfort increased. We sat outside a small building drinking coffee and smoking. I felt like an animal in a zoo. Circles of students formed thick bands of bodies around our table. Ali, Mustapha and Talib enjoyed the attention as they exhibited their catch.

To my horror, Ali had saved the greatest surprise until our arrival. I was to join them in their classes. The only good news of the day arrived when a disappointed looking Ali divulged that we had come on the day of German language lessons and I could not be used as a teaching aid. I tried hard to seem disappointed.

The four of us sat in the back row of the class. We all stared out of the window, idly watching builders cement a wall on the neighbouring house. 'Look see there,' Ali snapped out of his '*Eine, zwei, drei*' pointing to two girls and two young men walking across the construction side. All four mischievously hurried away. Ali tutted to himself.

'They are missing classes to be with their boyfriends. Imagine how much trouble they would be in if their fathers saw them now?'

By lunchtime we had finished the German lecture. I felt momentarily relieved as we left the university only to be informed that we would make our presence known at another. The three were keen to extract their full weight of social kudos from their new found asset. We paraded around a large courtyard surrounded by three levels of students inquisitively staring down at the foreign anomaly.

* * *

Sex. That was the most interesting topic to focus the attention of the three students. Obviously, it is an issue close to most young men's hearts, but in Syria, as well as much of the Middle East, sex had an occult-like status. It was a forbidden fruit that everyone wished to taste.

The hardest challenge was premarital sex. This needed a rebellious nature in both parties. It was a subject spoken of in hushed voices, nearly as taboo as talking about politics.

In the afternoon, we sat in a coffee shop smoking a waterpipe of delicious Bahraini sweet cherry tobacco. Blowing a voluminous cloud of smoke up to the ceiling, Ali tapped my arm, pointing outside the café. The same two girls we had seen from the German lecture, were now walking past the roundabout. They giggled together. Ali jumped to the most juicy conclusions. His voice revealed his jealousy.

'I can imagine what they will be saying to their parents. How they had been working hard with their studies. It would be a cover up for going and having sex with their boyfriends.'

Again Ali tut-tutted. His upper pallet and tongue clicking together.

'As you know, Charlie, most people here are Muslims. For a girl to have sex with a man before marriage is very bad. Still it goes on. Lots of people do it. Many of my friends have sex, but they are playing a game with death.'

I asked the rules of this deadly game. Ali gave a detailed score board analysis.

'If a man and a women are suspected of having sex. The girl's brother might kill that man. This isn't rare. We hear of it often. But the girl's brother will usually get into a lot of trouble. He might be put in prison for many years. However, if the brother actually catches them having sex, then killing the man will not be a problem. The girl's brother would be a witness and if he did go to prison, it would only be for a few months.'

I asked Ali about the level of police engagement in honour killings.

'The police try not to get involved. Well, not out here anyway. They will, if someone makes a big fuss. Usually, on both sides, the families will not want to talk about the incident. A family's honour and respect will be damaged.'

I asked Ali what was to be the fate of a woman in such circumstances? He looked uneasily at the floor. Ali understood European values. He seemed embarrassed.

'You must understand. The woman has made a huge mistake. She is unclean, and she will have damaged her family's reputation. If she is lucky, she may only be beaten, but in other cases, she too could be killed by her brother.'

I looked around at all three. They were staring at me for my reaction. Ali continued, predicting my next question.

'The police do nothing. It is a matter for the family and the girl, not the government. People will respect the family a lot more if the girl is killed. They will say the girl's brother is a real man.'

We left the coffee shop. Mustapha and Talib went home. Ali and I walked around a splashing water fountain. After a while, Ali felt sufficiently relaxed and with the others gone, he opened up a little more.

'I have had sex with a girl. She is my next door neighbour, but afterwards I learnt she has had sex with more men than just me.'

I asked Ali how he had achieved this, given the inherent difficulties.

'I was at home. I was alone. The house was empty and she asked if she could use our phone. I warned her that I was alone in the house, but she said that she didn't mind. That was how I knew she wanted to have sex. So she came around and it happened … but you see … **she's still a virgin.**'

We stopped walking and sat on a bench gazing at the yellow illuminated water that sprinkled out from the water fountain. I asked him an unfair question, as the response was entirely predictable. 'Ali, after you had sex with the girl, did you ever think about marrying her?' He looked at me in total disbelief. 'No, of course not! What are you thinking? She is unclean. I need someone pure.'

The town's nightlife was contained to a single street named 'Quarter to 6'. Neon lights flashed along an avenue of newly cobbled pavements. Behind the expensive flashy shops, the streets were dark and unhappy. We passed an old lady lying on the road outside her front door. She looked dirty and lonely. Ali hissed for my attention.

'You see her? She used to be the Parliamentary representative for Dayr Az Zawr. She would represent the town in Damascus. Her son hated the government and he got into trouble fighting in the underground movement. So one day, she received a parcel. Inside was his head. Ever since then she has been crazy. She just shouts, criticising the government.'

He chuckled to himself. 'She is our famous parliamentary lady.'

We walked down the street as Ali waved to numerous acquaintances and pointed out the local landmarks recalling past stories.

Next to the dilapidated state-run cinema, Ali subtly pointed to an undistinguished mobile phone shop. 'Look at this shop. It is owned by a hooker. She sells her body. But, it is hard to be a customer. People have to go through an agent.'

I asked Ali whether the women's family would ever find out. He looked at me with a disappointed face. Had I not learnt anything?

'Everyone knows she is a hooker. No one can go up to her

family and tell them. But, you are right in a way. She was worried about this and she knew she was getting a bad reputation so she started wearing a *chador*, but why? It makes no difference, she is still a hooker. She makes a lot of money … it's a good business.'

A Phoenician transvestite

Beirut, Lebanon
April 19

Individual passengers looked at one another, united in irritation. Our minibus would not leave Homs until the required additional two passengers materialised to fill the vacant seats.

A young man and his mother soon arrived and doors were slammed shut as we hastily departed across the border to Beirut. The young man noticed the sole foreigner and turned around from the front seat to touch my arm unnecessarily and introduce himself. I then answered the standard questions of where I was from and what I was doing in Syria before reciprocating.

'I'm Syrian. I'm going to Beirut with my mother. We're going to see my boyfriend.'

I thought I had misheard him. From my questioning face, he repeated himself. 'No, to see my boyfriend.'

I was shocked by his unshaken honesty. Despite not being able to relate to his plight, I was impressed by his courage. He was the first openly gay man I had met on my journey. This was hardly surprising as he was an oddity, representing the cultural antithesis of the region.

He let out a campish giggle in celebration at my surprise.

* * *

A few hours later, I arrived in Beirut and was sitting in a bar with my host for the night, Jason, an ex-naval officer who had come to the city to write for the *Daily Mail*.

My 'camp' companion from the drive to Lebanon was the first of many experiences over the next twenty-four hours that broke the supposedly ubiquitous conservatism of the Middle East. Beirut proved to be a law unto itself.

The evening was a loose memory of expensive bars and exotic women, or rather lack of.

Beirut has long been known as the 'party capital of the Arab world,' but nothing prepared me for the extravagance and opulence of Rue Monnot. The street had formerly been part of the 'Green Line' that separated the Muslim sections of East Beirut from the Christians in the West. After the civil war, snipers were replaced by bars and clubs dedicated to Beirut's nocturnal hedonism. Jason considered himself a competent womaniser after many nights spent charming the regulars of Rue Monnot and gladly accepted the role as my guide.

'It's all about image here. Even the Lebanese who don't have any money will still go out and blow a wedge. Lots of men will hire BMWs and Ferraris for the night simply to impress everyone with their leased status symbol.'

We passed cars that buzzed under the strength of their

bass boxes shaking in the boot. Their underslung neon lights illuminated pavements as they drove by.

'And the women. Christ! They are stunning.' Jason felt the need to demonstrate his great powers of persuasion. We passed a woman leaning aloofly out of a bar, smoking. He attempted to attract her attention.

'Hi, how's it going?' Regrettably, she ignored him, and purposely looked the other way. We carried on in silence and surveyed groups of steroid-driven men wearing dark sleeveless shirts with tight Armani jeans and metro-sexual offerings of jewellery. The women walked with a man on one arm and a concoction of French designer handbags on the other. Sunglasses were a requisite accessory against the night's bright lights, concealing heavily made-up faces from passing unsightly mortals. Jason and I slotted into this category of two portly Englishmen failing dismally to interest the mesmerising Lebanese women. These tantalising creatures had a unique appeal with their mysterious complexion of unblemished light olive-bronze skin, flowing black hair, high cheek bones and bright inquisitive eyes. I was realistic in my expectations. Jason was determined. He persisted where others would have given up.

Before hitting the nightclubs, our final bar stop was the 'Bunk Buster Bar' where customers sat on the floor leaning against sandbags, surrounded by mortar rounds and deactivated landmines that atmospherically poked out of the walls. Every surface had been painted with military patterns. Barbed wire separated enclaves around upturned ammunition boxes which acted as tables. I took a small anti-tank launcher from the wall and unwisely started to play with it. I pulled out the telescopic body. With an abrasive grinding noise, the metal cylinders extended into a long tube.

Jason looked around uninterested. I replaced the weapon on its wall mount while he lifted his glass, sinking his pint.

'Come on. This place is dead. We're going.' I followed the Lieutenant-Commander.

* * *

We headed up Rue Monnot once more, and followed a thudding beat down a dark staircase to a subterranean club.

Faces were concealed in the club's black and red décor. The barman was leaning across his bar between the legs of six women who were dancing belligerently to an Arabic rhythm. Their stiletto heels swung wildly knocking recently purchased drinks to the floor.

In the smoky haze of the dance floor, a circle had formed around a cavorting individual. I entered the hot mass of bodies to see the spectacle. The 'cavorter' wore tight black leather trousers and bright pink knee high boots, pouting lasciviously at the intimate audience. Had I missed the point? She was not a particularly attractive woman, yet men and women alike were drawn to her melodramatic dancing. I looked more closely at her face and saw the bumps of stubble underneath the camouflage of make up. Noticing my attention, she or he as I had come realise, wiggled over to me to speak in a loud, excited voice.

'Hi, I am Teddybear!'

To my and her surprise, I said nothing and could only nod in acknowledgement.

The figure turned and winked before her pink boots mingled back into the crowd of inebriates.

Module 6:

General studies

Marmite and American identity.
A dichotomy of love and hatred

Sana'a, Yemen
December 16

Yemeni traders sat behind their wares, tucked away in a small square that led off from Sana'a's boisterous Qat market of hypertraders and eager customers. The square was a more relaxed setting filled with plastic barrels and woven sacks spilling open with grain, rice, dried chillies and lentils. Large tobacco leaves hung in their dozens, suspended from rafters above. The air was perfumed by a touch of *eau de stale* cigarettes and damp vegetation. The afternoon sun spilled into the square casting long rays of light over the floating dust. Lines of exhaled tobacco rose neatly from the traders' seats. Their smokey jet streams broke to form a smoothly rising cloud.

In the nicotine-imbued ambience, I pressed my nose to tobacco leaves and sniffed eagerly. There was a delay as the venomous smell induced a sensual breakdown of sneezes and watering eyes. Unmoved, the tradesmen looked on curiously through their tobacco-enriched screen. They smiled at the Englistanee's foolhardy ignorance. Back out on to the streets, the crisp evening air helped to restore my lungs.

Leaning over some black rails to catch my breath, I spotted a father and his son kneeling down together, picking along a well-organised line of vegetables in a fecund garden that twisted around the dry wadi road. It was a common pastoral sight in the numerous urban gardens: parents squatting under palm trees educating their children in the finer points of domestic agriculture.

My attention turned back to the street as I heard the distinctive sounds of spoken English. It was not only the language which was so surprising, but the native English accents. The voices stopped, I turned around to see where the sounds came from. Two Western girls began to walk past me in silence. The taller of the pair concealed her black hair behind a red *hijab* with a bright red coat. Her accomplice chose a Shangri La-inspired hippy garment that rose to cover her head. I caught Red Coat's eye as they passed.

'Are you Tod?' she said.

'No. Sorry I am not. Should I be?' came my abrupt reply. I instantly kicked myself, as my solitude had misplaced the most basic of social graces. They did not seem taken aback. We started chatting and it transpired that this 'Tod' was a fellow 'gap year student', a British eighteen year old, who had moved to Sana'a to learn Arabic for a year.

After confirming my own identity and the accompanying disappointment that I was not the more desirable Tod, the girls introduced themselves as Rebecca and Sophia, Arabic students from Edinburgh University who took morning Arabic classes at a local school. They had found out about the infamous Tod's existence on the foreign students' grapevine. Unbeknown to Tod, he was being welcomed into their circle of friends.

'So what do you do all the time apart from language school in the mornings?' I asked.

Red Coat Rebecca, was the first to reply.

'I got a job at a local English-speaking newspaper. I just went and asked if they had any jobs and they gave me one on the spot. It's easy to get a job here as a foreigner. They love us for some obscure reason.'

Privately I thought that such love was hardly 'obscure' in her case. The reasons were clearly discernible as she stood smiling attractively, despite the shield of a red headscarf.

'Well, look. It's my birthday tomorrow and we are having a party.' Sophia interrupted my silent admiration. 'Come along? It's my twentieth.'

Slightly too eagerly I accepted, as optimism conjured up the most unlikely of outcomes.

'Great I'll show you the house.' We walked away from the bazaar and through the old city's indistinguishable streets. The girls walked confidently in the style of locals who had mastered the city's geography. We arrived at a shrinking alley that ran down to a small metal door opposite a minute food stall.

'Here it is. Just knock on that door tomorrow night, around 8 o'clock and we'll see you then.' Sophia had correctly judged my sense of direction. 'Oh, and remember that mosque as a landmark. Bye then.'

I watched them walk back into the winding streets that soon engulfed the two most attractive girls I had seen for weeks.

* * *

The next night, outside my hotel, a wedding reception was in full swing. A thick wall of men chanted Arabic wishes of marital prosperity and an abundance of children to the bridegroom. The stalwarts stood encircling a timid-looking man who seemed not to share their ebullience. His nervous hands clutched a straight, long **razha** sword. His eyes seemed to be transfixed in terror on the white wedding tent, where somewhere inside his new found nemesis awaited. I felt sorry for him as he was about to meet his future wife who at that point was a total stranger and a chosen partner of a union where his opinion had not been sought or required. The wedding night was yet to come.

The square was illuminated by bands of small white lights suspended through and between the trees. Small children rushed around with a disregard for the appearance of their smartest clothes, their mothers following them with a fear of scuffed shoes and grass-strained trousers.

Leaving the wedding in full swing, I made my way to the birthday party. The old city fell under a silent curfew. Only clipping footsteps of lonesome men and the meowing of feral cats could be heard around the winding streets. The light sky was cloudless. The moon shone strongly, giving enough light to show where blue and red Arabic graffiti squiggled across the grey stone street masonry. Approaching the 'landmark' mosque, I heard the sound of muffled hip hop attempting to breach Sana'a's thick walls.

The metal door was unguarded. I entered and went up a staircase to the epicentre of the party. There was a small kitchen which acted as the bar. My eyes widened at the sight of so many bottles of spirits, wine and beer. The floor had been lacquered with a sticky pool of residue spillage.

The party was a cosmopolitan gathering of Arabic students

from all corners of the globe. The Spanish contingency made their attendance known as they crashed into the kitchen stamping on piles of plastic cups beneath their feet.

In the next room, cushions had been placed along the walls, where a dozen people sat chatting, drinking, smoking and chewing Qat.

'Hey, you made it!'

'Happy birthday,' I said passing her a pot of Marmite which I had been parochial enough to carry with me since England wrapped in protective duck tape. Sophia was excited beyond the formalities of manners and appeared ecstatic by this odd gift.

'No way! Thanks. Oh my God, Rebecca! Look at this! We've got some Marmite. That's the best present I've had.' I tried to sound witty by explaining I thought there couldn't have been a local Marmite outlet this far south of Dover. Sophia thanked me endlessly. It was rather touching to see such devotion to this salty English spread. Only the anglophiles among the other foreign students knew what lay beneath the yellow lid.

'Where did you get all this booze from?' I asked Sophia.

Alcohol slowed Sophia's thoughts as she considered the question.

'It was a nightmare. We had to drive for two hours out of Sana'a to some hidden-away little garage that sold the stuff ... apparently it all comes from Egypt.'

Soon more guests arrived and she left me to greet them.

I sat up against the wall and chatted to Mark, a British graduate who had chosen Yemen as the venue to start a career in journalism. The famous Tod soon arrived with blond surfer hair and tired jeans. The three of us sat in a semi-circle as Tod and I pompously congratulated each other on our choice of gap year destination over the more traditional Bangkok and Melbourne route.

A group of rowdy Americans had flocked around the window sill, arguing over what music to play from a precariously placed laptop that looked dangerously close to falling out of the window. A tall, meagre-looking man came over to offer us all some of his Qat. On seeing him, Mark recounted the sort of story that forces Americans to attach deceitful Canadian flags to their rucksacks.

The Qat-offering American had recently shot to instant fame among the foreign students of Sana'a when his life had been threatened outside the old city gate, Bab Al-Yemen. His only crime was to have been too overtly American. On hearing Mark, he interrupted the story to give a first-hand account.

'Yeah, man that was bad. Well, basically, some Yemeni came up to me and said Hi! and asked me where I was from. And you know what? I'm not going to hide the fact that I am American. Right? I mean why should I? So anyway, I told the man that I'm American. He like looked at me as though I just badly insulted him. And then he said, 'If I ever see you again I'll kill you'. He stopped and shrugged his shoulders.

'So what did you do?' I asked.

'Well, a friend of mine saw what was going on and he called the police and the man got in a lot of nasty trouble for it. So it's cool now.'

A second American student had made more visible attempts to disguise his identity and took it upon himself to adopt a more advisory role.

'You've got to watch out for yourself here. Look at all this stuff I'm wearing.'

Like Lawrence of Arabia, he sat in the corner of the room concealed in local dress. He had chosen a black *dishdasha* with a grey headscarf and an uncomfortable looking green-sheaved **Khanjar** dagger that protruded from his midriff. The effect seemed only partially successful. I doubted whether his white complexion would not be noticed by suspecting Yemenis.

'So you wear that to avoid being seen as a foreigner?' I asked.

He looked irritated by my obvious question.

'Oh course, I wear this facade so no one's going to think I am a Yank.'

Two people come to terms with death

Aden, Yemen
December 7

I was stuck in Yemen. My credit card had been blocked in Oman and I had little money remaining. The various ways to reach Egypt were shrinking. Red tape, the plague of the twenty-first century, stopped me hitching a lift with one of the many oil tankers from Aden to Egypt's Port Safaga. My chances of convincing an unlikely private yacht to allow me safe passage up the Red Sea was stretching the realms of possibility.

My only overland hope lay in travelling by road up to Saudi Arabia and then west to the Red Sea ports where I could find passage across to Egypt. Yet the Saudis were not in the mood to help stray adolescents pass across their border. Firstly, due to the continuous *Shia Houthi* insurgency along the Saudi–Yemeni border and, more recently, the day before had seen a terrorist attack on the American Consulate in Jeddah.

In my depressing predicament I wandered over to the

British Consulate in a vain attempt to get some official recognition with which to harass the uncompromising Saudis.

Sitting in the bland waiting room was an elderly Yemeni and a man I presumed to be his son. I interrupted our silence. 'May I ask if you're a British citizen?'

The old man nodded. 'Yes. I moved from Aden to Manchester in the 1960s, and been there ever since. Now I am back here on holiday to see my old family again, but unfortunately we have had a tragedy.'

After a quiet pause he carried on, in the past tense.

'My son was born in Britain and ... he was obviously different from the average Yemeni. Last week he was driving alone from Aden to Sana'a when some men stopped the car to talk to him. He must have told them that he was British and on holiday as they pushed a Kalashnikov through the window and shot him ... He died two days ago.'

His wrinkled hands held open a maroon British passport. On the final page, a young Arab smiled behind the plastic screen.

I offered my condolences. He thanked me.

'You must be careful. It is not safe here in Yemen. Always watch yourself and don't take any silly risks. My son could at least speak Arabic. You are at a disadvantage.' The young man next to him looked at us silently with inquisitive eyes during our exchange. The old man turned to him.

'This is my nephew. He does not speak much English. But, he is very good at football and I am helping him get a visa to come and work in the UK.'

At that moment, I was called into another room and turned to wish them both luck. The consulate was run by the ever jubilant Mr Rajamanar who sat behind his desk with a great Cheshire cat smile. I told him about my situation. He rootled around in his desk, found the requisite pen and paper, and set about writing out an explanatory letter in Arabic.

'Charlie, I would be surprised if you do get a visa for Saudi Arabia. For one, the Saudis don't like people passing near Medina and Mecca, and secondly they are on alert after the recent attack on the American Consulate. As an employee of the British Consulate, I cannot officially help you on your trip to Saudi. This is against Foreign Office policy. Personally, I wish you the best of luck.'

I walked back out into the heat and the headed for the neighbouring Saudi Consulate. Two guards sat comatose under a tree.

'No. No one can come across the Kingdom of Saudi Arabia at this present time. Why don't you fly?'

Down and out, I crossed the dusty road to a grocery store. While mulling over the choice of chocolate bars, my mobile phone started to ring. The Devon area code flashed up on my Nokia screen. It was my mother.

'I've got some bad news.' I stood there bone stiff. Somehow I knew exactly what she was going to say. 'Last night, very peacefully, Grandpa died.' After 'last night' I stopped listening. Her words fell on deaf ears. 'He went to bed at nine and the nurses checked later that all was well. Then the morning nurse came to wake him up and found he had died in his sleep.'

My throat felt hoarse and cramped as though I was being strangled. My reply was a mere whisper. I felt a strange floating sensation around my body. I thought back to our last meeting. He was sitting in the nursing home watching Wimbledon before raising his hand to cover his eyes when Tony Blair appeared on the 6 o'clock news. I had uttered my last words to him, 'I'll see you when I get back.' He was more realistic than me and replied with the words, 'Just don't forget me.'

Ten seconds for 43,000 lives

Bam, Iran
October 8

It did not take a seismologist to realise that Bam was completely different from any other Iranian city. Ricardo, a Portugese IT consultant, and I stared out of the bus window in amazement. As we reached the outskirts of the city, Red Cross signs of Farsi scrawlings welcomed us to Bam. The placards announced 'Bam is recovering', the sort of 'it's not quite as bad as it looks', messages. Wiping the condensation off the window, I peered into the darkness. The road ran along a solemn path through a vacuum of mud rubble that spread out into the night. Occasionally, the odd wall or cracked house stood defiantly challenging the 6.6 Richter magnitude earthquake which had ravaged the city on December 26, 2003.

As with 60 per cent of the city, the bus terminal had ceased to exist. The bus hissed to a standstill by the Arg square roundabout. Climbing down the bus steps, the two of us stood by the side of the road hailing a taxi. I flicked through my guide book searching through a list of pre-earthquake hostels. Ricardo held a torch as we called out names of non-existent destinations.

Finally the taxi driver spoke. 'Ah, yes, OK. Akbar ... Akbar good'. Ten minutes later, we stood outside the once prominent 'Akbar's Guesthouse'. A tired-looking sign welcomed us to an empty plot. The elderly English teacher, Akbar stood by a tiny building no bigger than a small minivan. Around this minute house, Red Crescent and Oxfam tents had been erected for paying guests.

'I am sorry but a tent is all I can offer you now. This room here is for my family.' Looking across the vacant plot, the guesthouse's former foundations were now covered in a smooth layer of concrete. Two palm trees sprouted from an island of oozing mud. 'This was once the courtyard.' Akbar corkscrewed his hands, illustrating the former levels of his livelihood.

'After the earthquake, two metres of rubble was all that was left here. I had to clear it all with my own hands and now I must rebuild what I once had.' He stopped lamenting and looked back to reassure his customers. 'But do not worry. The new guesthouse has water, electricity and I have three extra tents if they are needed.' Ricardo and I nodded in agreement before climbing on to unsteady camp beds for the night.

The next morning, the two of us followed the routine tourist trail towards Bam's 2000 year old citadel, Arg-e-Bam. Only in the morning light, could we fully comprehend the extent of Bam's destruction. The city was a patchwork of vacant plots. Where houses once were, the ubiquitous Oxfam tents now stood alongside UN latrines and showers.

As we walked along the roads, hollow rebar-steel foundations rose from the ground like little wooden sticks from a plate of hors d'oeuvre. The earthquake had rendered the buildings flat, yet pockmarked with holes like a sieve. In the seismic flurry, bricks and cement had been shaken free leaving a lonely lattice of twisted metal.

Little children competed on their motorbikes in a death-defying game of harassing tourists. Ricardo and I had been unwittingly enlisted to play. Our ignorance was not important as there seemed to be no rules other than not to hit a tourist directly. A colonnade of 12 year olds would tactically approach before the winner and his following competitors tore past yelling a concoction of 'Hello.! Thank you! Yes sir!' Ricardo and I then fell to the ground as though seeking cover from a barrage of Messerschmitts. Sadly, this was much to the amusement of our adversaries who turned to laugh at their ditched victims.

The city was awash with the mechanical refuse of inoperable cars that lay abandoned on the side of the road. Their chassis had been twisted, rooves depressed, wheels buckled. It gave the city the appearance of having just fallen prey to an invasion of giant spiders which now lay shrivelled up in their deceased state.

Other vehicles were more of the walking wounded than the crushed tin can variety. A green BMW moved lethargically past us, the front passenger's side had been so depressed that the roof now touched the dash board. The driver accommodated the warped shape and drove with a Quasimodo panache, his head and neck peering out of the window.

Northeast of the city centre, we came to Arg-e-Bam, the old city of Bam. The site of the citadel had been originally built by a Sassians ruler, although before the earthquake most of the citadel had been the remains stemming from the later Safavid period. The city was of great importance as a Zoroastrian pilgrimage site and remained occupied well into the 1850s, acting as a key commercial hub along the East's famous 'silk road'.

A yellow prefabricated room marked the entrance to the citadel. There was an unmanned desk where tickets had once been issued. No soul appeared to sell, let alone officiously inspect our tickets of entitlement.

We walked along a raised scaffolding walkway above the crumbling remains that looked like a vast colony of termite mounds. The loose wooden planks rattled as we made our way and momentarily rocked, as we stepped over the occasional fulcrum.

The ancient citadel had been constructed entirely out of clay and mud bricks interlaced with straw and palm tree trunks. Mud-baked walls had crumbled like a line of dominoes, falling sideways and inwards upon one another. Other sections of the city projected upwards to the sky. It was like an image of an eruption of acne with irregular bumps of light brown mounds.

The citadel's main doors had been saved from collapse by reinforced wooden scaffolding. On the west wing, complete halves of rooms sat lopsided. Looking into the open rooms, I could make out calendars and pictures from the time of tourists. I held out my guidebook and glanced back and forth between a photo of the mystical citadel that once was, and the unrecognisable, anonymous face of rubble set against the blue sky.

Yet despite all this, old Arg-e-Bam still retained some of its Aladdin-like charm. The thick walls of the inner city still posessed two strong-looking turrets that stood like defensive props against a backdrop of green palm trees. There was even a governmental will to see the citadel reconstructed to its former splendour.

Leaving the sad citadel, Ricardo returned to Akbar's and I navigated onwards to the city centre on an outdated map that did not take into account the loss of landmarks. As nearly all the city was in decay, it seemed that only the famous date palms of Bam continued to flourish. The road to the city centre passed through date plantations full of trees clad with blue Christmas baubles. The 'baubles' were supermarket bags which covered thick green stems where a network of shooting branches held a bundle of luscious dates. The crop's annual success is due to Bam's ingenious interconnected deep wells which provide a balanced irrigation system under the city.

Arriving at the old bazaar, the ground followed the obvious lines of original paths and rough brick foundations where the stalls had once stood. As a modern alternative, aid organisations had come up with the pragmatic idea of using metal shipping containers as replacements for stalls where traders might sell and store their wares. I found an internet café near the bazaar. It seemed to epitomise the city. I sat in front of an uncommunicative computer and asked the owner for a coffee. He looked at me dumbfounded. 'No coffee here and internet, not working.'

* * *

Back at the hotel, Akbar sat outside chatting to Ricardo at a small wooden table. 'Compared to everyone else, I am a lucky man. Yes, some of my friends were killed, but no one in my immediate family. But in Bam no one remains unaffected. You know over 43,000 people died? I will never live to see this city as it used to be. My grandchildren? Perhaps, but me? I'm too old.'

In my peripheral vision, I spotted some movement of people creeping hap-hazardly up the road towards the guest house. As they drew closer I saw a Western couple. They were making slow progress because their pace was hindered by a man walking in front of them, filming the couple with an enormous camera on his shoulder. Behind them followed the second half of the film crew, with a man balancing a heavy microphone. Akbar saw them and stared with a worried face.

'Who are they, Akbar?' I asked.

He did not respond. He stared at the Western pair who were obviously filming some sort of documentary. The group reached the grounds of the 'hotel'. The woman spoke with a French accent, as she approached Akbar.

'Akbar, do you remember us? We are the French couple who were staying in your hotel the morning the earthquake struck.'

Akbar looked at them nodding, his eyes filling with tears.

Fadhi from a better life in Fallujah

Muscat, Oman
November 20

Ordering a Heineken, I stood by the bar in a cowboyesque fashion with one foot on the metal railing, chomping salty carrots. The bar had its own attraction, a *Sunni* Iraqi musician, Fadhi. Short and skinny, he had a rodent-looking face, but an attractive smile that put all his colleagues at ease. I was making up for lost time and as such getting to know the bar staff rather well. Prearti, the Philipino barman was foremost in holding Fadhi in deep respect.

'Among Arabian singers, there is not another man as nice as Mr Fadhi.'

I never discovered how many 'Arabian singers' Prearti had met before making such a comparison, but the two of them ruled the bar of the minute Al-Raha Hotel.

Fadhi had come to Oman after fleeing from Falluja which had been, quite simply, in his words, 'Bad for business.' Fadhi's business had been to play for a host of interesting individuals in the pre-invasion Iraq. He was rather matter of fact about his audiences.

'Well, I played a lot for Saddam Hussein's family. I never played for him personally, but my band played at his cousin's parties. They were bad parties. Saddam's cousin would always have lots of girls.' The tyrant was deemed innocent, as Fadhi continued. 'Saddam never did any of this.'

I pushed him a little further. Fadhi seemed unfazed when I asked him, 'Did you play for Uday and Qusay, you know, Saddam's sons?'

Fadhi looked at me with a disapproving expression. Clearly, he thought my question was mildly patronising. 'Of course I know who Uday and Qusay were. I never played for them but I had met them in nightclubs in the past. They were very bad people. If they liked a girl they would simply take them and force them to have sex. No one could touch them. Once Uday came up to my friend in a nightclub, and he asked my friend to do this.' Fadhi bent the little finger on his left hand and held it a few inches from his ear.

'Then Uday pulled out his gun and placed it around my friend's finger. Uday pulled the pistol firing shots next to my friend's ear. The bullets smashed all the mirrors on the wall. It was a huge mess, he smashed everything up, and my friend was very scared.'

Our conversation moved to less surreal topics as Fadhi pointed to my newspaper and the front page dominated by a large picture of an American soldier standing over an Iraqi body.

'Who are these people? They think that because they are American they are the most powerful and therefore the best. You see this?' Fadhi pointed to the picture: 'This is all part of Bush's *jihad*.' He searched my face for agreement.

'Don't you remember? Bush said the war in Iraq was a 'crusade' against Muslims.' This was one example of the public relations damage the poorly placed word had inflicted on America's image in the Middle East. Fadhi continued, 'I don't like the Americans. When I was at home in Fallujah, I was coming home from a restaurant and an American soldier pushed me to the ground and stamped his foot on my head. He then pointed his gun here.' Fadhi pointed to his temple. 'Then he shouted at me, 'Go home, go home!'

'However, the English, they are good.' He grabbed my wrist and made a cutting motion with his index finger. 'You see the English know that you and me, we have the same blood. We are all humans. The English are a decent people and that is why Basra is a peaceful place in comparison to Baghdad. I know why the Iraqi people like the English. Like you, we have tea and cake everyday at 4 o'clock in the afternoon.'

I asked Fadhi about life pre-invasion in 2003. He surprised me with his response. I imagined the US-led invasion would have been a welcome change. Fadhi raised his eyebrows and slowly rocked his head.

'Life was very good. I made a lot of money. I would earn at least $200,000 a year. I owned a furniture factory, as well as playing music. I used to take lots of vacations to Beirut and Egypt. Business was great. Life was great.' He stopped talking and shook his head again, but this time in disapproval. 'Then the war started and business wasn't good. No one bought my tables and my factory had to close. Everything became expensive. I was rich and even I could only afford one loaf of bread a day. I could not buy cigarettes. One pack cost a $100 US.' He chuckled to himself. 'Every day, I thank President Bush. He helped me stop smoking.'

He shrugged his shoulders while recollecting, 'Before the

war, life was easier. Cigarettes did not cost $100 US. It was cheap to live in Iraq. It used to cost 25 cents to fill up a car. Electricity and water costs were very cheap, now the water is dirty and the electricity never works because the Americans have bombed our power plants.'

* * *

I said little not wishing to interrupt his tirade.

'And the Americans accused Saddam of possessing 'weapons of mass destruction'. Where are the 'weapons' now? George Bush is a great liar.'

Fadhi ceased his rantings, calmly sipping lemonade as all good Muslims do, unlike his later clientele who preferred more illicit concoctions.

The nightly connection between alcohol and Arabs provided a certain bizarre amusement. While I was waiting for my Yemeni visa, I occupied my days with second rate films and reading **Lorna Doone** before coming to the bar every night to see Fadhi under the hot blast of stage lights, as he simultaneously sang and played at two mounted keyboards. Three Moroccan dancers would mill around half-heartedly shuffling and twirling their hands. Their faces were so heavily made up one could almost make out cracks, as with parched soil. The oppressive heat had dried out their masks. Their shiny nylon dresses glistened as they oscillated. Michelin tyres of fat protruded from lazy midriffs that moved in seismic waves to the tinny Arabic music. It was not a pretty sight. But I was alone in my opinion. Omani men sat alone in unblemished white **dishdashs** ogling the spectacle. Cigarettes hung in abeyance with drooping ash curved into overflowing ashtrays. Beckoning hands would call over the Indian waiters, half-ashamedly conspiring for another beer. The single occupants of each table peeped around to the next. Each man a sinner, held a glass in one hand, tut-tutting in disapproval to other offenders who in turn reciprocated the admonishment of alcohol to the initial aggressor.

Al-Raha Hotel was Oman's closest equivalent venue to *Stringfellows.* It was a wonderfully hypocritical scene. Only in this slightly seedy bar could men ogle at the exposed feminine form, a pleasure society publically prohibited.

As the nights passed, I got to know Prearti. Initially, not knowing where the three prima ballerinas came from, I asked Prearti their origins, over the booming twang of synthesiser guitars. Prearti looked at me with an amused expression. Like a teacher gently correcting his mischievous pupil, he shook his head and wagged his finger at me, tugging at his clothes with the other hand. He leant forward and bellowed in my ear:

'No. They are dancers only. They are not prostitutes. I am sorry.'

I was reluctant to accept this apology for fear of cementing his misinterpretation that I was fishing for a more private dance. I made the mistake of trying to explain myself. Prearti was increasingly amused by my pleas of innocence and soon told the other waiters.

The next night I sat down at my usual table nearest the bar where a beer and a bowl of peanuts were waiting. The table had been reserved with a small cardboard plaque placed upright against the stem of the beer bottle. I could make out the black biro scribble: '*Proustitate*'.

Entering Yemen with Julia Roberts

Al-Hawf, Yemen
November 26

The taxi sped through huge dry wadis of wedding cake-layered hills. Cracks ran down the hillsides like winter's chapped lips. Red flags poked up over crevasses indicating the Omani army's firing ranges. Down on Mughsail beach, fisherman brought in their morning catch, their long banana-shaped wooden boats bobbing in the lapping waves of the Arabian seas. Camels idly walked across the road with little concern for anyone or anything. Beeping car horns seemed unable to faze these great beasts of the desert, whose thick serpentine necks glided back, as big eyelashes blinked to see who was in such a hurry.

From the road, scrubby bushes emerged over the harsh landscape. Their twisted and deformed shape had been skillfully sculptured by the weather. Branches and leaves had been forced, bent into one direction as the prevailing winds dictated. Looking out of the car window, I imagined frankincense and mysterious African Boabab trees lying hidden among the local flora and fauna. In minutes, the landscape changed from the scrubbish unfertile grasslands to steep tropical hills covered with densely wedged trees. A few miles north lay the blinding white sands of Rub Al Khali, the Empty Quarter.

I found it difficult to contain my excitement. After two months in 'civilised' Oman, I was finally moving into the feral nation of Yemen. My mind raced to discover what exactly happens in Yemen, a land only travel writers seemed to have remembered. Like the Congo might have seemed to past explorers, Yemen was to my mind a blank spot on the map. This was a nation with whom I had already fallen in love and felt drawn towards. The expats of Oman had largely been shocked by my plans. Many times I endured lectures about the 'black-listed country' of Al-Qaeda tribesmen who sharpened daggers while waiting in ambush for fair-skinned Christians.

Such scepticism made Yemen even more desirable. An ingrained curiosity and sheer stubbornness kept me pursuing an elusive Yemeni visa. Yemen was like Tiverton on a Wednesday afternoon at school, 'out of bounds'. But Yemen was not the same as bunking off a rugby match and escaping to the **White Ball** for an illicit pint. Yemen was to me the ultimate border to be breached, the great unknown that begged to be explored.

* * *

The ink had not even dried on the neat 'Sarfait Border Post' stamped into my passport as I left the Omani border, when a sickly feeling hit my stomach which started to churn like a dying cement mixer. I felt the old nausea of previous attempts to access Exeter nightclubs under-age. The schoolboy heroism had worn off. I was scared. I flicked my toes for the reassurance of $1000 US wedged in a sock.

A shabby rusty sign welcomed me to Yemen. Upturned oil barrels, smashed breeze blocks and loose plaster rubble from a collapsed wall blocked the left hand side of the road. It was a sharp contrast to the clean painted border post of Oman. I had walked twenty metres and found myself in the ultimate third world country. A dozen men and teenagers sat on a balcony smoking and pouring cups of hot black sweet tea down their gullets. They surveyed me somewhat coolly.

'You Americeezee,' one pointed and muttered.

I quickly made it firmly understood that I was most definitely *not* 'Americeezee'. Thankfully one of their colleagues got it right, shouting out 'Britannia, Britannia' as my passport went around the group like some worn trophy while they all flicked through it. Heads nodded indicating that all had understood the Latin alphabet and the foreign English words. The group were more academic than oral in their English linguistic skills as few spoke more than a couple of words.

We soon hit a wall as my Arabic formalities were insufficient in bartering safe passage further into this isolated border hinterland. I sat in silence for 15 minutes. Soon, a jolly fat man appeared and put everyone at ease, welcoming me to Yemen and pouring another cup of tea. His great beard shook when he spoke. He had sensed my caution.

'Do not be worried by Yemeni people. They are good.'

Misjudging the moment, I poured out to my uncomprehending audience some rubbish about the unjust media portrayal of Yemen. They all nodded in polite agreement.

Despite my arrogance in ignoring the Omani expat

mandate, I was becoming increasingly nervous. There was no escaping the fact that Yemen was a harbour for Al-Qaeda suspects, with tribesmen who held the reputation for kidnapping tourists. My mind battled with competing insecurity and subsequent reaffirmation that I was doing the right thing. My main fear centred on the possibility of being refused entry and being tossed back into Oman.

Attempting to suppress my fears, I drank yet more tea and smoked countless cigarettes. I focussed on the border guards, observing their motley ways. Taking the great explorer Wilfred Thesiger's lead, I too found them to be handsome and smartly dressed men. A creaseless sarong fell from their waists just covering the knees. Equally creaseless, long-sleeved shirts gave the collective group assembled an air of officialdom. Individuality lay in the headscarf as all wore a different headcloth in his own way. Others pulled their headdress apart, leaving little superhero capes that hung from their shoulders, the triangular point perfectly aligned with their vertebrae.

The border area was a rubbish site. In the multifunctional carpark-come-rubbish tip, no patch escaped withered plastic bags which also fluttered on the pointy Dhofar trees. Cigarette butts were showered around like confetti, appearing like lice crawling in heady tufts of green grass. Naked window frames opened on to bare rooms. Bollocks to those unnecessary things like furniture and electricity. This was Yemen and it was going to be kept simple.

Quite suddenly, a small Suzuki jeep hand-braked and skidded around the grass-come-gravel car park. A short soldier arrogantly leaped out of his chariot. His military beret hung unevenly on his head.

'Mr Charles? We go.'

Sitting in the front passenger seat, my vision was obscured by my rucksack on my lap for lack of anywhere else to place it. In the back, one poor soldier winced in agony as he squatted down, sandwiched behind a huge boxed television. Subduing my feeling of insecurity, we travelled away from Oman and into the forgotten Yemen. The conceited driver shared the same passion as most Iranians seem to have when driving. He clearly had a death-wish and attempted to crash whenever the opportunity arose, making a great effort to drive on the wrong side of the road, a phone in one hand and my passport in the other. He succeeded in calling three people while narrowly avoiding a head-on collision with a 5-ton military truck packed with young soldiers.

The road snaked downhill and we came to the most eastern seaside village in Yemen named 'Al-Hawf'. The jeep pelted up a rickety dust track between scraggy houses. We bumped along the uneven track before accelerating to an abrupt stop. My lunatic chauffeur jumped out, pulled my rucksack off my lap, handed me my passport and indicated I should get out. With that, he swiftly drove off.

* * *

I squinted around at my surroundings in the afternoon sun. In front of me spread Al-Hawf, a village of breeze blocks and orange plaster that glowed with a rouge haze. At the foot of the village, the sea shimmered in a diamond-shaped blanket of sunlight. Along the beach, children extended in a file of long lines out to sea. They stood diagonally from one another, pulling in long fishing lines. Black blocks of women waited on the golden sands to free the squirming catches from knotted nets. Their topless sons and husbands bobbed up and down trying to get a foot on the uneven sea bed.

My rucksack swung with momentum as I turned around to find myself standing outside a small brown fort. The building seemed like a ghost town. I walked into a dusty courtyard. Lots of little rooms ran off along to the sides. Something creaked behind me. I turned to see four men who had patiently watched me for the last few minutes. They sat silently up against a wall on an old metal bed frame. Their mattress was a frail straw mat, and they propped themselves up with revolting dirt-engrained pillows. Their Kalashnikovs acted as arm rests, leaning against the wall. We stared at each other, then looked on motionless like gazing chameleons. Their left cheeks bulged out as though the four were all member of a family menaced by hereditary mouth tumours.

Of the four, one stood out, 'Joker' as I came to call him. He wore a red and white headscarf with an olive green *dishdash* that fell to his ankles. From a matching green belt was suspended a battered curved golden *Kanjar* knife. Joker led the ritual passport inspection. Joker's superior, a grey-haired old man, groaned, pointing to my Iranian visa before dramatically throwing his arms up. Using my black biro scribbled map, I pointed out my path from Istanbul to Salalah.

The green Suzuki military truck which my driver had attempted to martyr earlier on, pulled into the courtyard. A chorus of 'Julia Roberts' spilled out as ten young men climbed out. I laughed to myself thinking that *Pretty Women* had made it to the little known coastal outpost of Al-Hawf. However, I did not wish to be associated with Hollywood actresses and more importantly, Americans. I pointed to my chest repeating, 'Englizee, Englizee, *min* (from) London.'

Joker was bored with talking about American actresses and was in his element reeling off jokes at my expense. He looked at me before reaching the punch line and laughed loudly with his colleagues, slapping his thighs in self-congratulation.

Then, with a psychopathic change from humour to horror, Joker looked stone faced and tried to bait me by pointing at the hills surrounding Al-Hawf opposite the coast.

'Bin Laden, yes, Osama Bin Laden … he come.' He pointed away from the hills to me before dragging his finger across his throat in a slitting gesture. Joker's behaviour only fuelled my fears. Once again, I viewed myself as the worthless infidel, whose government and state-established heretical religion sponsored Zionist 'pigs' in a continuous crusade against Muslim brothers and sisters.

Just as abruptly, with another twist of personality, Joker abandoned his call for Bin Laden to take my life and smiling kindly, handed me a chilled bottle of mango juice.

I was never certain of Joker's sincerity, but his recent actions supported other instances I had experienced during my travels in the Middle East. Although I may embody all the things Joker disliked, I was still a guest in his country, and as such, he would welcome me with nothing but the best hospitality he could offer.

Moments later, a heavy lump fell on to my lap. I looked down to see a well-worn Russian pistol. Slowly pulling back the top slide, I could see a dull golden bullet, that lay like a little devil in the breech. From its evident ease, the pin was cocked. Joker took the gun back and relieved the magazine of further drops of death that lay stacked, waiting patiently to strike. After mango juice and a pistol, Joker promoted me to assault rifles, carefully laying down on my lap, a bulky Kalashnikov.

Due to the unconventional behaviour of the border guards,

I decided to test their level of unprofessionalism. I pointed to the Kalashnikov and then to the sky in a firing motion. Would they let me blast off a few rounds?

They united in a disapproving clicking of tongues.

Looking around my surreal surroundings, I noticed that it was not only the original four whose mouths were puffed up into large tumour-like bulges. Everyone dipped their mitts into black plastic bags and picked leaves off purple and green stems. Once plucked, the delicacies would be masticated gently and pushed to the left cheek. Saliva would bloat the leaves into a green ball that grew exponentially with each mouthful. This was my first introduction to Qat, an amphetamine-like plant of waxy leaves. The drug comes with the predictable health risk, but the Yemenis I met assured me that Qat was only a social stimulant which kept them mentally agile.

Joker was the first to hand me a clump of leaves. I followed their example picking the leaves and placing them in the side of my mouth. Their waxy outer coating slid on my tongue with a screeching rubber sensation. Biting the leaves released a revolting juice. The Qat was not acidic or peculiarly sweet, but had a bitter, dull, numbing, (dare I state the obvious?) 'leafy' taste. To me, Qat tasted no different from leaves in the average English garden, chewing such having been an unfortunate childhood pastime of mine. Despite having never been a committed hedonist I thought the drug was a great disappointment. It failed to fulfil its role and had no effect on me whatsoever. I was certain to thank Joker nonetheless and declined any more offers while surreptitiously spitting the green paste out on to the dusty floor.

Despite the exciting start of narcotics and firearms, I realised time was pushing on into late afternoon. I was quite happy to leave my new friends. The real boss had been hiding inside one of the small rooms running around the courtyard. Eventually he emerged, with a small girth and neat brown hair, explaining they were 'processing' my visa. The English verb 'processing' sounded a little too organised for Joker and his colleagues who 'processed' away in a room that lacked electricity.

Unlike his minions, the chief was a friendly man and squatted on his haunches to talk to me in broken English.

'I have been in London Embassy in 1964 … I go there for three months … ah a good place … Britannia very good … I like it and South Kensington … very nice place.'

On hearing this, I felt sorry for the man who had been exposed to the beauty and affluence of London only to end his career in the provincial border post of Al-Hawf. Minutes later, the chief handed me my passport. He smiled,

'Welcome to Yemen.'

I was ecstatic to receive his official blessing. Al-Qaeda, here I come.

* * *

A battered old Toyota Corolla taxi came to the fort and out stepped Ibrahim, a tall black African whose family had, at some time, crossed the Gulf of Aden. Standing there, he looked down on his Arab colleagues from his great height. His grey T-shirt had been proudly stencilled with the image of Saddam Hussein on the front. Small bombs fell above Arabic text that denounced the United States. Joker made sure I had not missed the political reference. I smiled and got into the back of the Corolla where three policeman sat compacted like sardines, their rifles pointed in a variety of directions. Joker added to our discomfort, hitching a ride into Al-Hawf central, and we set off down the rickety path.

Ibrahim briefly stopped on the coastal road. Young Yemenis sat in small cafés resting after bringing in the day's catch, smoking shesha waterpipes. A crowd soon surrounded the taxi. Joker, to my dismay, encouraged them, before getting out himself to say goodbye. He leant in through the window to show me his wallet. Instead of family pictures, Joker had chosen a more predictable individual on whom to shower his affection. Looking most military, Joker flaunted what seemed to be the regional pin up: two identical passport-sized pictures of his Excellency the former President of Iraq.

'Saddam, he was good man.' Joker grinned from ear to ear with a sadistic smile.

Module 7:
Final Exam

Failing the final assessment: drinks with Robert Fisk

Beirut, Lebanon
April 21

Other than learning that Garibaldi was not only a currant-filled biscuit worth accumulating at school concerts, I took time in my final year at school to approach everyone who I could associate with the Middle East.

I was very excited when a blue envelope arrived on the kitchen table one morning from the *Independent*'s Robert Fisk. His hand-written letter included contact details and an invitation to get in touch when I arrived in Beirut.

Nervously, I called him upon arrival. He vaguely remembered our correspondence and invited me to meet him that evening at the Riviera Hotel at 6.30 pm. 'Where was I staying?' came his question.

I hesitated. Despite worthy intentions and the literal interpretation, the American Embassy was not a diplomatic location in Beirut. I told him.

There was a long uncomfortable silence at the other end of the line. I broke the stalemate explaining that I was simply staying with a friend and had no political connections with the Embassy staff.

Apprehensively, he agreed to see me provided that I came alone.

I made my way down to the Corniche and saw the only Caucasian man outside the hotel. Fisk greeted me coldly and turned to walk ahead of me along the pavement past lines of bullet-ridden palm trees. At a large block of flats, an old wire cage lift took us up to his apartment. I was directed to the balcony where I waited in a big wicker chair, checking my notes. Above the black railings of the balcony, I could see the Mediterranean's gently rolling waves.

He reappeared with two tumblers and a bottle of red wine. Covered in a mixture of nerves and gratitude, I thanked him again for agreeing to see me.

'It's no problem. When I was your age, no journalist ever had time for me. So now, anyone who comes knocking usually finds an open door.'

During the next hour, I was able to test my knowledge and to gauge, through a stream of obvious questions, whether or not I had grasped a full understanding of the Middle East.

I started by asking Fisk what life was like as a correspondent in Beirut during the civil war? Smiling gently, he recounted various amusing and surreal aspects of life in war-torn Beirut. 'As I still do today, I used to live in Beirut's Muslim sector, but worked throughout the city. At the weekends I would go and see my Lebanese-Armenian girlfriend in Geneva. Every time I returned to Lebanon there was one smell that reminded me of Beirut, the smell of rubbish burning in the street. After a few years it was hard to contemplate anywhere that wasn't in a permanent state of war. Life just carried on.' He smiled. 'I even used to go to the cinema during the civil war.'

Prior to meeting Fisk, I had heard numerous criticisms about his supposed lack of professionalism. Despite his extensive international profile, many thought that his years spent in the region, covering the Arab–Israeli conflict, had eroded his impartiality as a journalist. His work was dismissed by many as a litany of pro-Palestinian diatribe.

Taking heed of this, I tactfully mentioned my recent visit to the Palestinian refugee camp Shatila the day before. He instantly saw the reasons for my cautious approach and with a wry smile summarised the hopeless situation for Palestinian refugees in Lebanon with a brief history lesson. This was based on the fact that according to the UN General Assembly Resolution 194 in 1948, the Palestinians could all return to Palestine. However, as we all know, the General Assembly never had any real power and Israel never appeared to show any intention of complying with the resolution.

The tone of his voice became ironic as his recounted a past story to illustrate his point. 'A pro-Israeli American group once came to Lebanon in an attempt to resolve this problem and return the Palestinians to Galilee. The Israelis were in despair. The group had not realised that the old Palestinian villages had become Israeli settlements. There is simply no space for the Palestinians anymore, even if the Israelis ever did comply.'

I asked Fisk about the version of Ariel Sharon's involvement in the 1982 Sabra and Shatila massacres. A point Nasim, the Palestinian-Danish taxi driver, had incorrectly recounted. Nonetheless, a subsequent Belgian criminal court case attempted to try Sharon in 2001 for his involvement in the massacres. Fisk gave a brief reply to the effect that the events had happened and could not be changed, that Donald Rumsfeld had made a hasty appearance to the court and had put a stop to it.

Rather than dwelling on the past, Fisk wished to press on me what could be changed in the present. His interests lay in the new generation of Palestinians and what little Lebanon had to offer them.

'I have an old friend in Ireland at Trinity College who offered to accept some bright Palestinians on a graduate-scholarship programme. I have a young Palestinian friend here, in Beirut. He speaks perfect English and like everyone else wants to emigrate out of Lebanon. But he creates problems for his case as he is so adamant in insisting on taking his family with him, especially his sister. It's what all of the Palestinians want. They simply want to leave this country.'

From the apartment, we could see the charred remains of the St George Hotel, the site of the former President Hariri's assassination. Expressionless, Fisk looked out at the fading sky before turning his attention to Hariri's demise and his own close shave.

'I was close enough to the blast without it being fatal. I had slipped on some coffee in the kitchen and damaged my spine. Doctors at the American hospital told me to carry out some light exercises. Following their orders I was walking along the cornice on February 14th when the bomb exploded. I was knocked to the ground. When I got up, I ran over to a cloud of dusts rising from the bomb site.' At this point, I interrupted him mid-story.

'But weren't you scared of a second bomb?'

'Yes, but I carried on walking until I came to the crater where people were staggering around covered in blood. I saw a man I recognised but could not remember where from. He was one of Hariri's bodyguards. He staggered over to me, saying 'Mr Fisk, the big man is gone.' I thought he meant that Hariri had gone to hospital, then realised he had meant that Hariri had, Yalla, gone, to heaven. On the pavement, I saw the severed hand of a woman. A wedding ring was still attached to one finger. Later, I found out that she was the wife of a doctor I had once met. It was a very sad day for Lebanon. I had personally known Hariri well.'

Hariri's death further pressurised the withdrawal of Syrian forces from Lebanon, a legal requirement after the earlier UN Resolution 1559. The third clause of this resolution also called for 'the disbanding and disarmament of all Lebanese and non-Lebanese militia.' This was primarily aimed at Hezbollah and I considered it to be an obvious policy that would push the factions of Lebanese society to the table rather than the front line should likely disagreements reoccur in the future.

My views were not shared. Fisk dismissed such calls for disarmament as too simplistic. 'Two nights ago, I was at a party in a house where the host kept a Kalashnikov. I am the only one on my block without a weapon. When weapons are not needed, they are not used. They become obsolete, useless. Asking people to disarm just creates further unnecessary friction, confusing any serious peace efforts. Asking Hezbollah to disarm is nothing short of asking them to surrender, and why should they do that?'

In a roundabout way, we returned to Resolution 1559's main clause calling for the withdrawal of foreign forces from Lebanon, notably Syrian forces, who had already withdrawn. Again, in my mind, this made complete sense. Lebanon, as with all nations, should be guardians of their own future, should they not?

'Come here.' I was jovially ordered into the living room. He stood searching among many picture frames that hung from the wall. He showed me a small framed print. Wearing their blue pointy hats, French revolutionary soldiers rowed wooden boats into a harbour. I read the words at the bottom of the picture 'Beirut, Syria.'

As Fisk pointed out, Western powers have been involved in Lebanese affairs for centuries. Before the Sykes-Picot treaty, Lebanon was part of Greater Syria. Today, in Tripoli in Northern Lebanon, up to 40–50 per cent of the people are Syrian and many even have Syrian passports. The two countries are and have been permanently entwined. So is it surprising that Syria has maintained a strong presence in Lebanon? Fisk concluded, 'For many Syrians, Lebanon is simply another Syrian province.'

It must have been like work for him to have to explain the basics of history and politics to an uninformed audience of one. I put down my notepad of illegible scrawls and asked him about a famous episode in Afghanistan when he was attacked when visiting a village. He was matter-of-fact about the event. 'American B52 bombers had targeted the wrong area creating appalling devastation. Many people had lost their entire families. A huge crowd of men had gathered and encircled me before punching and kicking me to the ground. I remember staring at a bus, thinking to himself, 'how long does it take to die?' Then I remembered a young Lebanese girl who, in 1976, told me that the worst thing to do in such a situation was to do nothing at all. So I took her advice and got up and started hitting back at the Afghans. I can remember the crunching noise of bone as I broke someone's nose and even smashed a few teeth.' I was invited to look at the war scars. He held his hand to the light, pointing to two small incisions of Pashtun teeth marks on the back of his knuckles. Without any hint of heroism, he continued. 'Suddenly it all ended when an imam moved into the centre of the crowd and pulled me out.'

Fisk turned his focus back to Rafiq Al Hariri. 'Hariri heard about the incident in Afghanistan and called me, offering to fly me back to hospital in Beirut in his private jet, but I could not accept a favour from a politician, and had to turn down his offer.'

By this stage, I had taken two hours of the famous correspondent's time and thought it wise to know when to leave. I stood up to go and he walked through the apartment to see me out. At the door, he opened up and was even paternal in his words.

'I don't want to put you off becoming a journalist. But you have to realise it's not some game of flashing cameras and awards. You actually have to live these wars. Living them will affect every aspect of your life, including the people you love. A lot of foreign correspondents start off thinking they are mere observers of someone else's troubles. A bulletproof jacket will only protect you from bullets. It's not an easy life. Events still affect you years later.'

Taking the stairs down to the street below, I was consumed with anger at myself, coupled with self pity.

Before meeting Robert Fisk, I had imagined our conversations to be my final assessment of all I had experienced during my travels in the Middle East. Fisk was, unwittingly, my examiner. I had failed. I had not 'cracked' the Middle East. It had not been a case of going there, seeing the issues, understanding the facts and reaching the 'correct' conclusions.

It was not that I assumed I should agree with Fisk on all matters, but the evening had exposed something I had previously tried to suppress and ignore. My increasing familiarity with the region had bred a complacency in my own opinions.

My methods of assessment had been crude and infantile. With everything new that I read, experienced and judged, I had often looked at it all with a preconceived idea of the rightful outcome, often ignoring the debate.

That evening, for the first time I realised that despite what one reads, however many people one meets, one can never know the absolute truth about an event, a history, a country or a people. One can only aspire for an awareness of the confusions and complexities of life.

But it was exciting too. In those two hours, I had had my enlightenment.

I realised that the competing claims upon history cannot be ranked in grid positions for dominance over the direction of the future. History is not a series of chronological events that fluidly follow reason or logic. The extent and depth of emotions cannot be quantified and measured. Not everything can be analysed according to the set format of an essay plan.

At that moment walking down the Corniche, I realised that this was far from the end of an education. This was just the beginning.

Inshallah.